The Secret History of Intelligence Operations

Shah Rukh

Published by Shah Rukh, 2024.

While every precaution has been taken in the preparation of this book, the publisher assumes no responsibility for errors or omissions, or for damages resulting from the use of the information contained herein.

THE SECRET HISTORY OF INTELLIGENCE OPERATIONS

First edition. July 12, 2024.

Copyright © 2024 Shah Rukh.

Written by Shah Rukh.

Table of Contents

Prologue

In the shadowy realm of intelligence and espionage, truth is often stranger than fiction. This hidden world, shrouded in secrecy and deception, has shaped the course of history in ways most of us can scarcely imagine. From ancient empires to modern superpowers, the covert actions of spies, codebreakers, and covert operatives have played crucial roles in the rise and fall of nations, the outcome of wars, and the delicate balance of global power.

This book, "The Secret History of Intelligence Operations," seeks to unveil the clandestine operations that have defined eras, influenced geopolitical landscapes, and left indelible marks on the annals of history. Each chapter delves into a unique and true case of intelligence or espionage, bringing to light the extraordinary stories of those who operated in the shadows. These narratives reveal the remarkable ingenuity, courage, and sometimes the moral ambiguities of the men and women who have worked behind the scenes, often risking their lives in the pursuit of information and power.

We begin with Operation Mincemeat, a masterstroke of deception during World War II that saved countless lives and altered the course of the war. From there, we explore the labyrinthine codes of the Enigma machine, the audacious maneuvers of the Cambridge Five, and the dramatic capture of Adolf Eichmann by the Israeli Mossad. Each chapter offers a window into a different facet of intelligence operations, from covert assassinations and elaborate deceptions to high-tech cyber warfare and the complex world of counterintelligence.

As we journey through these remarkable stories, we uncover the hidden dynamics that have driven some of the most pivotal events in history. The intelligence community operates on the razor's edge, where success and failure are often separated by the thinnest of margins. The stakes are immense, and the consequences of these secret battles reverberate far beyond the immediate targets and operatives involved.

"The Secret History of Intelligence Operations" is not just a collection of thrilling tales; it is an exploration of the human spirit, the lengths to which individuals and nations will go to protect their interests, and the ethical dilemmas that arise in the pursuit of secrecy and knowledge. It is a testament to the ingenuity and resilience of those who have operated in the shadows, shaping the world in ways that are both profound and, until now, largely unseen.

As you turn these pages, prepare to enter a world where nothing is as it seems, where deception is an art form, and where the truth, though often obscured, is always lurking just beneath the surface. Welcome to the secret history of intelligence operations.

Chapter 1: Operation Mincemeat: The Deceptive Corpse

Operation Mincemeat was one of the most audacious and successful deception operations of World War II, orchestrated by the British to mislead Nazi Germany about the Allies' plans for invading Southern Europe. The brainchild of British intelligence officers Ewen Montagu and Charles Cholmondeley, Operation Mincemeat involved an intricate scheme that revolved around planting false information on a dead body to mislead the enemy. This elaborate ruse was designed to convince the Germans that the Allies intended to invade Greece and Sardinia, rather than the actual target of Sicily.

The operation began with the selection of a suitable corpse. Finding a body that appeared to have died from drowning without any signs of trauma was crucial for the operation's credibility. Eventually, they found Glyndwr Michael, a homeless man who had died from ingesting rat poison. His body was preserved and prepared to play the role of Major William Martin of the Royal Marines. The transformation of Michael into Major Martin involved creating an elaborate backstory, complete with personal documents and love letters to add authenticity. The corpse was dressed in military uniform and provided with an attaché case containing fabricated top-secret documents. These documents were meticulously crafted to suggest that the Allies were planning to invade Greece and Sardinia, with Sicily being merely a diversion.

The next challenge was to ensure that the body would be discovered by the Germans. To achieve this, the corpse was placed in a canister and taken aboard the submarine HMS Seraph, which set sail for the coast of Spain. The choice of Spain was strategic, as it was neutral but known to have strong German intelligence presence. On the night of April 30, 1943, the body was released into the waters off the coast of Huelva, where it eventually washed ashore. The Spanish authorities discovered the body and, as anticipated, informed the Germans about the discovery of the "drowned British officer."

The success of Operation Mincemeat hinged on the Germans taking the bait and believing the false information. The British intelligence had ensured that the planted documents would make their way through the Spanish channels to the Germans. The Germans, convinced of the documents' authenticity, altered their defensive strategies. They diverted significant forces to Greece and Sardinia, weakening their defenses in Sicily. This diversion played a crucial role in the success of the Allied invasion of Sicily, which began on July 9, 1943. The invasion, codenamed Operation Husky, caught the Germans off guard, leading to a swift and decisive victory for the Allies. The success of Operation Mincemeat was a testament to the ingenuity and meticulous planning of British intelligence. The operation not only saved countless Allied lives by easing the invasion of Sicily but also showcased the effectiveness of strategic deception in warfare.

The impact of Operation Mincemeat extended beyond the immediate tactical advantage. It demonstrated the power of misinformation and psychological warfare, reshaping intelligence operations in the future. The operation became a classic example of how deceptive tactics could influence enemy decision-making and change the course of the war. In the years that followed, the details of Operation Mincemeat remained classified, known only to a select few within British intelligence. It wasn't until after the war that the full story began to emerge, capturing the imagination of historians and the public alike. The operation was later immortalized in the book "The Man Who Never Was" by Ewen Montagu, which provided an insider's account of the daring deception. The story of Operation Mincemeat also served as a reminder of the sacrifices and ingenuity of those involved in intelligence operations during the war. It highlighted the lengths to which the Allies went to secure victory and the pivotal role of covert operations in achieving strategic goals.

The success of Operation Mincemeat can be attributed to several key factors. The careful selection of the body, the creation of a convincing backstory, and the meticulous preparation of the false documents were all crucial elements. Additionally, the understanding of German intelligence procedures and the strategic placement of the body ensured that the deception reached the intended audience. The operation also benefited from the broader context of Allied intelligence efforts. The establishment of the Twenty Committee, a group dedicated to deception operations, provided the necessary resources and coordination for such complex schemes. The committee's work extended beyond Operation Mincemeat, contributing to other successful deceptions throughout the war.

In retrospect, Operation Mincemeat stands as a remarkable example of creativity and daring in the realm of intelligence. It showcased the potential of unconventional tactics to achieve significant strategic outcomes. The operation remains a subject of study and admiration, illustrating the enduring importance of deception in military strategy. The legacy of Operation Mincemeat continues to influence intelligence operations to this day. The principles of deception and misinformation it exemplified are still relevant in modern warfare, where the battle for information and perception plays a critical role. As such, Operation Mincemeat is not just a historical anecdote but a lesson in the power of strategic ingenuity and the enduring impact of intelligence operations.

Chapter 2: The Enigma Machine: Cracking Nazi Codes

The Enigma machine, an intricate and sophisticated cipher device used by Nazi Germany during World War II, stands as one of the most iconic symbols of cryptography and wartime intelligence. Developed by German engineer Arthur Scherbius at the end of World War I, the machine was initially intended for commercial use, but its potential for military applications quickly became evident. The German military adopted the Enigma machine in the 1920s, and it became the cornerstone of their secure communications, used extensively by the Wehrmacht, Luftwaffe, and Kriegsmarine.

The Enigma machine was a marvel of engineering, featuring a complex system of rotors, plugboards, and wiring that created an astronomical number of possible encryption combinations. Each machine had three to five rotors, depending on the model, which could be arranged in different orders and set to different initial positions. The rotors, each with 26 positions, interacted with one another to scramble plaintext messages into seemingly indecipherable code. The plugboard, or steckerbrett, added another layer of complexity by allowing pairs of letters to be swapped, further increasing the number of possible settings. The sheer number of possible configurations—estimated at 150 quintillion for a three-rotor machine—made breaking the Enigma code appear impossible.

However, the Allies recognized the critical importance of deciphering German communications to gain a strategic advantage in the war. The effort to crack the Enigma code became one of the most significant and secretive operations of the war, involving a collaborative effort across several countries and a cadre of brilliant mathematicians, cryptanalysts, and engineers. The journey to breaking the Enigma began with the work of Polish cryptanalysts in the early 1930s. Marian

Rejewski, Jerzy Różycki, and Henryk Zygalski, working at the Polish Cipher Bureau, made significant progress in understanding the Enigma machine's mechanics. They developed a method for reconstructing the machine's internal settings and created a replica machine known as the "bomba kryptologiczna." Their groundbreaking work provided the first major breakthrough in the Allied efforts to break the Enigma code.

With the looming threat of war in 1939, the Polish cryptanalysts shared their findings and techniques with their British and French counterparts. This crucial exchange of information laid the foundation for the code-breaking efforts at Bletchley Park, the British Government Code and Cypher School located in Buckinghamshire. Bletchley Park became the epicenter of the Allied cryptographic efforts, where some of the brightest minds of the time, including Alan Turing, Gordon Welchman, and Dilly Knox, gathered to tackle the Enigma problem. Alan Turing, a mathematician and logician, played a pivotal role in the effort to break the Enigma code. Turing's insight into the mathematical principles underlying the Enigma machine led to the development of the Bombe, an electromechanical device designed to expedite the code-breaking process. The Bombe was capable of rapidly testing different rotor settings, significantly reducing the time required to find the correct configuration for a given day's Enigma settings. This innovation, coupled with other techniques developed at Bletchley Park, enabled the Allies to read a substantial portion of German communications.

The successful decryption of Enigma-encrypted messages provided the Allies with invaluable intelligence, known as Ultra. Ultra intelligence encompassed a wide range of information, from tactical battlefield orders to strategic plans and movements of German forces. The ability to read these messages allowed the Allies to anticipate German actions, counter their strategies, and make informed decisions that ultimately contributed to the success of numerous military operations. One of the most notable impacts of Ultra intelligence was during the Battle of the Atlantic. German U-boats posed a significant threat to Allied shipping, and the ability to decode Enigma messages allowed the Allies to track and evade U-boat wolf packs, significantly reducing losses and ensuring the vital flow of supplies across the Atlantic. Ultra intelligence also played a crucial role in the success of Operation Overlord, the Allied invasion of Normandy in June 1944. By decrypting Enigma messages, the Allies were able to mislead the Germans about the location and timing of the invasion, contributing to the success of D-Day and the subsequent liberation of Western Europe.

Despite its monumental success, the work at Bletchley Park remained shrouded in secrecy for many years after the war. The codebreakers' contributions were not publicly acknowledged until the 1970s, and the full extent of their achievements only became widely known in the decades that followed. The secrecy surrounding Bletchley Park was a testament to the importance of intelligence and the need to protect the methods and sources that provided such a decisive advantage. The legacy of the Enigma machine and the efforts to crack its code extend beyond the immediate impact on World War II. The work at Bletchley Park laid the foundations for modern computing and cryptography. Alan Turing's contributions to the development of the Bombe and his theoretical work on algorithms and computation are considered pioneering steps in the field of computer science. Turing's ideas about machine intelligence and his formulation of the Turing Test continue to influence research in artificial intelligence to this day.

The story of the Enigma machine and the codebreakers who unraveled its secrets is a testament to human ingenuity, perseverance, and the power of collaboration. It underscores the critical role of intelligence in warfare and the profound impact that breaking enemy codes can have on the outcome of a conflict. The success of the codebreakers at Bletchley Park was not just a triumph of technology and mathematics, but also of creativity, innovation, and teamwork. In addition to its historical and technical significance, the story of the Enigma machine has captured the popular imagination, inspiring numerous books, documentaries, and films. Works such as "The Imitation Game," which dramatizes the life of Alan Turing, have brought the story of Bletchley Park and its codebreakers to a broader audience, highlighting their remarkable achievements and the ethical dilemmas they faced. The Enigma machine itself has become an enduring symbol of the complexities and challenges of wartime cryptography, representing both the formidable obstacles posed by secure communications and the relentless efforts to overcome them. As we look back on the story of the Enigma machine and the breaking of its codes, we are reminded of the enduring importance of intelligence in national security and the continuing evolution of cryptographic techniques in the digital age.

Chapter 3: Operation Fortitude: The D-Day Diversion

Operation Fortitude, a critical component of the broader Allied deception strategy during World War II, stands as one of the most masterful and elaborate misinformation campaigns in military history. Designed to mislead the German High Command about the actual landing site of the D-Day invasion, Operation Fortitude played a pivotal role in ensuring the success of Operation Overlord, the Allied invasion of Normandy on June 6, 1944. By creating the illusion of imminent attacks on other locations, Fortitude diverted German attention and resources, thereby facilitating a more effective and less contested landing in Normandy.

The operation was divided into two main parts: Fortitude North and Fortitude South. Fortitude North aimed to convince the Germans that the Allies planned to invade Norway, while Fortitude South suggested that the primary target was the Pas de Calais, the narrowest point between Britain and France. Each segment involved an intricate web of false information, deceptive military movements, and the use of double agents to feed misleading intelligence to the Germans.

Fortitude North focused on Norway, a region of strategic importance to the Germans due to its proximity to Britain and its role in securing northern shipping routes. The deception included the creation of a fictitious British Fourth Army, which supposedly amassed in Scotland. This phantom army was equipped with inflatable tanks, dummy landing crafts, and fake radio traffic to simulate preparations for an invasion. The Allies also staged training exercises and troop movements to lend credibility to the ruse. These efforts were complemented by the dissemination of false intelligence through double agents and controlled leaks, all aimed at convincing the Germans that an invasion of Norway was imminent. As a result, the

Germans kept substantial forces stationed in Norway, far from the actual invasion site in Normandy.

Fortitude South was even more elaborate and crucial to the success of the Normandy invasion. The primary objective was to persuade the Germans that the main Allied assault would occur at the Pas de Calais, rather than Normandy. The Pas de Calais was the most logical and expected invasion point due to its proximity to England and its suitable landing beaches. To reinforce this deception, the Allies created an entirely fictitious First United States Army Group (FUSAG), ostensibly commanded by General George S. Patton, who was highly respected and feared by the Germans. Patton's involvement added significant weight to the deception, as the Germans believed that he would lead any major invasion effort.

The creation of FUSAG was a masterstroke of deception. The Allies went to great lengths to simulate an entire army group, complete with fake headquarters, radio traffic, and even false troop movements. They employed various tactics, including the use of dummy tanks and aircraft, to create the illusion of a substantial military presence in southeastern England. The Allies also conducted visible but non-threatening reconnaissance missions and training exercises along the English coast opposite the Pas de Calais. These activities were designed to be observed by German intelligence, further reinforcing the illusion of an impending invasion.

The deception was further supported by the use of double agents, most notably Juan Pujol García, codenamed Garbo. Pujol was a Spanish double agent who had gained the trust of the Germans and was feeding them a mix of true and false information. His reports about the buildup of forces in southeastern England and the imminent attack on the Pas de Calais were crucial in convincing the German High Command of the veracity of the threat. Additionally, controlled leaks and fake intelligence documents were deliberately allowed to fall into

German hands, all pointing towards the Pas de Calais as the primary invasion target.

The success of Operation Fortitude hinged not only on the creation of convincing false information but also on the Allies' ability to control and manipulate the flow of information to the Germans. This required a sophisticated understanding of German intelligence operations and a careful orchestration of deception efforts across multiple channels. The Allies' ability to maintain the secrecy of their true plans while disseminating convincing falsehoods was a testament to their expertise in intelligence and counterintelligence operations.

The impact of Operation Fortitude on the success of the Normandy invasion cannot be overstated. By convincing the Germans that the main invasion would occur at the Pas de Calais, the Allies were able to achieve several key objectives. First, they ensured that the German forces in Normandy were not reinforced with troops from other regions, particularly the powerful Panzer divisions stationed in the Pas de Calais. This meant that the initial landings in Normandy faced less resistance than they would have otherwise.

Second, the deception caused the Germans to delay their response to the Normandy landings. Even after the Allies had established a beachhead in Normandy, the Germans continued to believe that the main invasion was still to come at the Pas de Calais. This belief led them to hold back their reserves and reinforcements, waiting for an attack that never materialized. This hesitation allowed the Allies to consolidate their positions in Normandy, build up their forces, and eventually break out from the beachhead.

Third, Operation Fortitude contributed to the overall success of Operation Bodyguard, the larger strategic deception plan aimed at misleading the Germans about Allied intentions in Europe. By creating a complex web of deceptions that included threats to Norway, the Mediterranean, and other regions, Operation Bodyguard helped to spread German forces thin and sow confusion among their commanders. Fortitude was a crucial element of this broader strategy, and its success was instrumental in the overall effectiveness of Allied deception efforts.

In the aftermath of the war, the details of Operation Fortitude and the broader deception efforts remained classified for many years. It was only in the decades following the war that the full extent of the operation was revealed, highlighting the ingenuity and creativity of the Allied intelligence community. The success of Operation Fortitude has since become a classic case study in the field of military deception and intelligence, illustrating the power of strategic misinformation and the importance of psychological operations in modern warfare.

The legacy of Operation Fortitude extends beyond its immediate impact on the outcome of World War II. The principles and techniques developed during the operation have influenced subsequent military and intelligence operations, shaping the way modern armed forces approach the use of deception and misinformation. The operation demonstrated the effectiveness of using false information to manipulate enemy decision-making, a concept that remains relevant in today's complex and information-rich battlefields.

Moreover, Operation Fortitude serves as a reminder of the critical role of intelligence in warfare. The success of the operation depended not only on the creation of convincing falsehoods but also on the Allies' ability to gather, analyze, and exploit intelligence about German capabilities and intentions. The operation underscored the importance of understanding the enemy's mindset and using that knowledge to craft effective deception strategies.

In popular culture, Operation Fortitude has captured the imagination of historians, writers, and filmmakers, inspiring numerous books, documentaries, and films that explore the intricacies of the operation and its impact on the D-Day invasion. These works have helped to bring the story of Fortitude to a broader audience, highlighting the bravery, ingenuity, and determination of those involved in the deception efforts.

As we reflect on the story of Operation Fortitude, we are reminded of the extraordinary lengths to which the Allies went to secure victory in World War II. The operation exemplifies the power of creativity and innovation in overcoming seemingly insurmountable challenges. It also serves as a testament to the enduring importance of intelligence and deception in the conduct of military operations. The success of Operation Fortitude was not merely a triumph of tactics and technology, but a demonstration of the power of human ingenuity and the relentless pursuit of victory against formidable odds.

Chapter 4: The Cambridge Five: Soviet Spies in Britain

The Cambridge Five were a notorious group of Soviet spies who infiltrated the highest levels of British intelligence during the mid-20th century. This clandestine network, composed of five British men—Kim Philby, Donald Maclean, Guy Burgess, Anthony Blunt, and John Cairncross—passed significant secrets to the Soviet Union, fundamentally altering the landscape of Cold War espionage. Their story is one of ideological commitment, betrayal, and the intricate web of intelligence operations that defined much of the 20th century.

The origins of the Cambridge Five can be traced back to the University of Cambridge in the 1930s. At this time, the political climate in Europe was highly charged, with the rise of fascism in Germany and Italy and the growing threat of another global conflict. Cambridge was a hotbed of political activity, and many students were drawn to leftist ideologies, seeing them as a bulwark against the fascist tide. Among these students were Kim Philby, Donald Maclean, Guy Burgess, Anthony Blunt, and John Cairncross, who would later become the core of the Soviet spy ring. They were recruited by Soviet intelligence during their university years, motivated by a mix of idealism, disillusionment with the British establishment, and a genuine belief in communism.

Kim Philby, perhaps the most infamous of the five, was recruited by Soviet intelligence in 1934. His charm, intelligence, and upper-class connections made him an ideal candidate for espionage. Philby's career in British intelligence began in the early 1940s, when he joined MI6, the British Secret Intelligence Service. He quickly rose through the ranks, eventually becoming the head of counter-espionage operations. In this position, he was ideally placed to pass critical information to his Soviet handlers. Philby's ability to mislead and manipulate his colleagues was extraordinary, and he successfully diverted suspicion from himself for many years. His tenure in British intelligence provided the Soviets with invaluable insights into Western strategies, particularly during the early years of the Cold War.

Donald Maclean, another key member of the group, joined the Foreign Office in 1935. His career included postings in Paris and Washington, D.C., where he had access to sensitive diplomatic and military information. Maclean's intelligence contributions were crucial during World War II and the early Cold War period. His access to top-secret documents allowed him to provide the Soviets with detailed reports on Allied strategies and post-war planning. Despite exhibiting erratic behavior that raised suspicions among some colleagues, Maclean managed to avoid detection for many years, in part due to the protective network provided by his fellow spies.

Guy Burgess, known for his flamboyant personality and unconventional behavior, was also a valuable asset to the Soviet Union. Burgess worked for both MI5, the British domestic intelligence service, and the Foreign Office, where his assignments included postings to Washington, D.C. His indiscretions and erratic behavior often drew attention, but his connections and charisma enabled him to evade serious scrutiny. Burgess's role as a courier for Maclean ensured a steady flow of intelligence to the Soviet Union. His eventual defection to Moscow, alongside Maclean in 1951, was a significant blow to British intelligence and a stark indicator of the penetration of Soviet espionage.

Anthony Blunt, an esteemed art historian and later the Surveyor of the Queen's Pictures, was another crucial member of the Cambridge Five. Blunt's access to high society and the British establishment provided a unique channel for Soviet intelligence. During the war, he worked for MI5, where he had access to highly classified information. Blunt's contributions were primarily in the form of detailed reports on British counter-intelligence operations. His espionage activities remained undiscovered until 1963 when he was confronted and confessed in exchange for immunity from prosecution. Blunt's revelation in 1979 caused a public scandal, particularly due to his royal connections and the leniency he had been shown.

John Cairncross, the fifth member of the group, worked in various government departments, including the Foreign Office, the Treasury, and the Cabinet Office. His intelligence work included providing the Soviets with critical information about British and American atomic research, including details about the Manhattan Project. Cairncross's espionage activities were less well-known compared to his counterparts, and he managed to maintain a relatively low profile throughout his career. His eventual exposure added another layer to the complex web of the Cambridge Five.

The impact of the Cambridge Five on Cold War dynamics was profound. The intelligence they provided to the Soviet Union altered the balance of power and influenced strategic decisions on both sides. Their espionage activities compromised numerous operations and endangered the lives of countless agents and operatives. The information they passed on covered a broad range of subjects, from military strategies and diplomatic communications to scientific research and technological advancements. The betrayal was a significant blow to British and Allied intelligence, leading to a reevaluation of security protocols and counter-espionage measures.

The discovery and unmasking of the Cambridge Five were a gradual and complex process. Suspicion first fell on Donald Maclean, whose erratic behavior and heavy drinking had raised concerns among his colleagues. In 1951, with the net closing in, Maclean and Burgess fled to Moscow, confirming their guilt and exposing the extent of Soviet infiltration. Philby, who had helped orchestrate their escape, came under intense scrutiny but managed to evade immediate exposure. It was not until 1963 that Philby was definitively unmasked as a Soviet spy. Faced with mounting evidence and fearing arrest, he defected to the Soviet Union, where he spent the remainder of his life.

The exposure of Blunt and Cairncross followed in the subsequent years, each revelation adding to the sense of betrayal and the magnitude of the intelligence breach. The British government faced intense criticism for its handling of the affair, particularly the decision to grant immunity to Blunt in exchange for his cooperation. The public and political fallout from the revelations of the Cambridge Five was significant, leading to widespread calls for reform within the British intelligence community. The scandal underscored the need for more rigorous vetting and monitoring of intelligence personnel and highlighted the vulnerabilities that could be exploited by determined and ideologically motivated adversaries.

The legacy of the Cambridge Five is multifaceted, encompassing both the profound impact they had on Cold War espionage and the broader lessons about trust, loyalty, and the complexities of ideological commitment. Their story has been the subject of numerous books, documentaries, and films, reflecting the enduring fascination with their exploits and the moral ambiguities they embodied. The tale of the Cambridge Five serves as a cautionary example of how deeply embedded spies can operate within a nation's most sensitive institutions, posing significant challenges for security and counter-espionage efforts.

In the annals of espionage history, the Cambridge Five stand out not only for the scale of their betrayal but also for the remarkable success they achieved in evading detection for so long. Their ability to operate undetected for decades speaks to the sophistication of their methods and the deep-seated ideological convictions that drove them. The story of the Cambridge Five continues to resonate, offering insights into the nature of espionage, the complexities of loyalty and betrayal, and the enduring impact of ideological conflicts on global security dynamics.

Chapter 5: The Zimmermann Telegram

The Zimmermann Telegram stands as one of the most pivotal and dramatic incidents in the history of World War I, profoundly influencing the course of the conflict and shifting the geopolitical landscape. Dispatched by German Foreign Minister Arthur Zimmermann in January 1917, this coded message was intended for the German ambassador to Mexico, Heinrich von Eckardt. Its contents proposed a military alliance between Germany and Mexico in the event that the United States entered the war against Germany. The interception and decryption of the Zimmermann Telegram by British intelligence, and its subsequent exposure to the United States, played a crucial role in tipping American public opinion in favor of entering the war. The ramifications of this single piece of communication were immense, ultimately contributing to the Allied victory and reshaping global politics.

In the early years of World War I, the United States maintained a position of neutrality, under the leadership of President Woodrow Wilson. While economic and cultural ties with the Allied powers were strong, there was significant opposition within the U.S. to becoming embroiled in the European conflict. Public opinion was deeply divided, with many Americans advocating for peace and isolationism. However, tensions began to escalate as Germany's unrestricted submarine warfare increasingly threatened American lives and commerce. German U-boats targeted Allied and neutral shipping, leading to the sinking of vessels such as the Lusitania in 1915, which resulted in the deaths of 128 Americans. This act of aggression significantly strained U.S.-German relations and sowed the seeds of American involvement in the war.

Amidst this volatile backdrop, the Zimmermann Telegram was sent. Germany, seeking to neutralize the potential threat of American intervention, devised a bold and audacious plan. The telegram proposed that Mexico should join forces with Germany against the United States. In return, Germany promised to support Mexico in reclaiming lost territories in Texas, New Mexico, and Arizona—regions that Mexico had ceded to the U.S. following the Mexican-American War in the mid-19th century. The offer was intended to distract and preoccupy the United States, keeping it bogged down in a conflict on its southern border and away from the European theater.

The British interception of the telegram was a stroke of extraordinary luck and skill. The British Admiralty's Room 40, a top-secret code-breaking unit, had been monitoring German communications since the early days of the war. On January 16, 1917, the British intercepted the Zimmermann Telegram as it was transmitted from Berlin to the German embassy in Washington, D.C. From there, it was to be relayed to Mexico City. The British cryptographers faced the daunting task of deciphering the message, which was encoded using a sophisticated cipher. Through a combination of cryptanalytic expertise, prior knowledge of German codes, and a bit of good fortune, the British succeeded in decrypting the telegram.

Upon realizing the significance of the intercepted message, the British faced a delicate diplomatic challenge. They needed to find a way to present the telegram to the United States without revealing their intelligence-gathering methods, which could compromise their ongoing surveillance of German communications. The British crafted a carefully orchestrated plan to disclose the contents of the telegram in a manner that would maximize its impact. They presented the decrypted message to the American ambassador in London, Walter Hines Page, who then relayed it to President Wilson.

The reaction in the United States was explosive. The contents of the Zimmermann Telegram were published in American newspapers on March 1, 1917, igniting a firestorm of public outrage. The audacity of Germany's proposal shocked the American public and galvanized support for entering the war. The idea that Germany sought to incite a neighboring country to wage war against the United States, with the promise of reclaiming American territory, was seen as a direct and unacceptable threat to national sovereignty and security. The telegram provided the decisive push that many Americans needed to shift their stance from isolationism to intervention.

President Wilson, who had been re-elected in 1916 on a platform of keeping the United States out of the war, found himself compelled to act. The Zimmermann Telegram, coupled with the continued threat posed by unrestricted submarine warfare, made it increasingly clear that neutrality was no longer a viable option. On April 2, 1917, Wilson delivered a momentous speech to a joint session of Congress, in which he called for a declaration of war against Germany. Wilson framed the conflict as a struggle for democracy and justice, stating, "The world must be made safe for democracy." Four days later, on April 6, 1917, Congress overwhelmingly voted to declare war on Germany, officially bringing the United States into World War I.

The entry of the United States into the war had profound implications for the conflict and its eventual outcome. American resources, manpower, and industrial capacity provided a significant boost to the Allied war effort. The influx of fresh American troops helped to tip the balance on the Western Front, providing much-needed relief to the war-weary British and French forces. The United States also played a crucial role in bolstering the Allied economies and maintaining the flow of essential supplies and munitions.

Moreover, the involvement of the United States had a profound psychological impact on both the Allies and the Central Powers. For the Allies, American entry into the war brought renewed hope and determination, reinforcing their resolve to continue the fight. For Germany and its allies, the prospect of facing the combined might of the United States, in addition to the existing Allied forces, was a severe blow to morale. The American presence on the battlefield and in diplomatic negotiations added significant weight to the Allied cause.

The Zimmermann Telegram's impact extended beyond the immediate military and strategic consequences. It also had lasting effects on U.S. foreign policy and international relations. The decision to enter World War I marked a significant departure from the United States' traditional stance of isolationism and set a precedent for future American involvement in global affairs. The war fostered a sense of international responsibility and leadership that would shape U.S. foreign policy throughout the 20th century.

In the years following the war, the Zimmermann Telegram continued to be a subject of fascination and study. Historians and scholars have analyzed the episode from various angles, exploring its significance in the context of wartime intelligence, diplomacy, and communication. The story of the Zimmermann Telegram is often cited as a classic example of the power of intelligence and the impact of cryptography on the course of history. It underscores the importance of effective communication and the potential consequences of its interception and decryption.

The legacy of the Zimmermann Telegram also serves as a reminder of the complexities and nuances of international relations. It highlights the interplay between diplomacy, intelligence, and public opinion in shaping the decisions of nations. The episode illustrates how a single piece of communication, when skillfully intercepted and strategically revealed, can alter the trajectory of global events. The Zimmermann Telegram remains a powerful testament to the enduring significance of intelligence and the profound impact of information in the modern world.

As we reflect on the story of the Zimmermann Telegram, we are reminded of the intricate web of human actions and decisions that shape the course of history. The episode is a compelling example of how individuals and nations navigate the challenges of war, diplomacy, and communication. It is a story of ambition, deception, and the unpredictable consequences of seemingly isolated events. The Zimmermann Telegram, with its far-reaching implications and dramatic revelations, continues to captivate our imagination and deepen our understanding of the complexities of the past.

Chapter 6: The Rosenberg Case: Espionage and Execution

The Rosenberg Case remains one of the most controversial and significant espionage trials in American history, reflecting the intense fear and suspicion that characterized the Cold War era. Julius and Ethel Rosenberg, a married couple living in New York City, were convicted of espionage for allegedly passing atomic secrets to the Soviet Union. Their trial and subsequent execution in 1953 not only polarized public opinion but also highlighted the broader themes of anti-communist hysteria, government secrecy, and the morality of the death penalty. The case's intricate details, political ramifications, and enduring legacy continue to provoke debate and reflection.

The backdrop of the Rosenberg Case was the heightened anxiety of the Cold War, a period marked by intense rivalry between the United States and the Soviet Union. The development and use of atomic bombs by the U.S. during World War II had established it as the dominant superpower. However, the Soviet Union's successful detonation of its own atomic bomb in 1949 shocked the American public and government, triggering a wave of fear about the potential spread of nuclear technology. The idea that American secrets could be stolen and used to build weapons of mass destruction by the Soviets was a terrifying prospect that fueled a widespread anti-communist sentiment.

Julius Rosenberg was an electrical engineer who had been a member of the Communist Party. His involvement in espionage began during World War II when he worked as a civilian engineer for the U.S. Army Signal Corps. Through his position, he had access to classified information which he allegedly passed on to Soviet agents. Ethel Rosenberg, his wife, was accused of assisting Julius by recruiting her brother, David Greenglass, into the espionage network. Greenglass, who worked as a machinist at the Los Alamos Laboratory where the atomic bomb was being developed, became a crucial witness for the prosecution after he was arrested and decided to cooperate with the authorities to secure a lighter sentence.

The arrest of the Rosenbergs in 1950 came at a time when the U.S. government, under the influence of Senator Joseph McCarthy and the House Un-American Activities Committee (HUAC), was aggressively pursuing suspected communists and sympathizers. The trial of Julius and Ethel Rosenberg in 1951 was a sensational event that captured national attention. The prosecution, led by U.S. Attorney Irving Saypol and his assistant Roy Cohn, painted the Rosenbergs as dangerous traitors who had put the nation's security at risk by providing the Soviets with vital information about the atomic bomb. The evidence against them included testimonies from Greenglass and other alleged co-conspirators, as well as documents that purportedly showed their involvement in espionage activities.

The trial was marked by intense media coverage and a charged atmosphere, reflecting the broader anti-communist sentiment of the time. The defense, led by attorney Emanuel Bloch, argued that the case against the Rosenbergs was based on circumstantial evidence and the unreliable testimony of witnesses who were seeking leniency for their own crimes. Bloch also contended that Ethel Rosenberg's involvement was minimal and that she was being prosecuted primarily to exert pressure on Julius to confess and name other conspirators. Despite these arguments, the jury found the Rosenbergs guilty, and Judge Irving Kaufman sentenced them to death, citing the gravity of their crime and its potential to hasten a global conflict.

The death sentence sparked a global outcry, with many people, including notable intellectuals, artists, and political figures, arguing that the punishment was too harsh and that the trial had been unfair. Protests and appeals for clemency poured in from around the world, with prominent figures such as Albert Einstein, Pablo Picasso, and

Jean-Paul Sartre speaking out against the execution. Critics of the verdict argued that the evidence against the Rosenbergs was insufficient to warrant the death penalty and that their prosecution was influenced by the pervasive anti-communist hysteria of the era. They also pointed to the fact that no other accused spies, including David Greenglass, had received the death penalty, suggesting that the Rosenbergs were being made scapegoats to send a message about the consequences of treason.

Despite the international pressure and numerous appeals, President Dwight D. Eisenhower refused to grant clemency, and the Rosenbergs were executed in the electric chair at Sing Sing Prison on June 19, 1953. Their deaths marked the first and only execution of civilians for espionage in U.S. history and left a lasting legacy of controversy and debate. The execution was a somber and divisive event that highlighted the deep divisions within American society and the broader implications of the Cold War.

In the years following the Rosenberg executions, new evidence and revelations have emerged that have further complicated the narrative. Declassified Soviet archives and the release of the Venona decrypts, which were intercepted Soviet communications, confirmed that Julius Rosenberg had indeed been involved in espionage activities and had provided valuable information to the Soviets. However, the extent of Ethel Rosenberg's involvement remains a subject of debate. Some historians argue that her role was minor and that she was largely prosecuted and executed to pressure her husband, while others contend that she was an active participant in the espionage network.

The case has also prompted broader reflections on the use of the death penalty, especially in cases involving espionage and treason. The execution of the Rosenbergs has been cited by opponents of capital punishment as an example of the irreversible and potentially unjust consequences of the death penalty. The moral and ethical considerations of executing individuals for espionage, particularly when the evidence may be circumstantial or based on unreliable testimonies, continue to be a topic of significant debate.

The Rosenberg Case remains a powerful symbol of the Cold War era, encapsulating the intense fear, suspicion, and ideological conflict that defined the period. It serves as a stark reminder of the potential for justice to be swayed by political pressures and the dangers of allowing fear to dictate legal and governmental actions. The story of Julius and Ethel Rosenberg is a complex and multifaceted one, reflecting the broader struggles of a nation grappling with issues of security, loyalty, and civil liberties in a time of profound uncertainty.

The legacy of the Rosenberg Case continues to resonate in contemporary discussions about national security, government transparency, and the balance between individual rights and state power. It is a case that invites ongoing examination and reflection, offering lessons about the dangers of political extremism, the importance of fair and impartial justice, and the enduring impact of historical events on the collective consciousness. The Rosenbergs' story is one that will continue to be studied and debated, serving as a poignant example of the complexities and contradictions inherent in the pursuit of justice in a world fraught with fear and conflict.

Chapter 7: The U-2 Incident: High Altitude Espionage

The U-2 Incident, which occurred on May 1, 1960, was a critical episode in the Cold War, highlighting the tension between the United States and the Soviet Union and the intricate world of high-altitude espionage. This event involved the downing of an American U-2 spy plane over Soviet airspace and the capture of its pilot, Francis Gary Powers. The incident dramatically exposed the lengths to which both superpowers would go to gain intelligence on each other, significantly impacting U.S.-Soviet relations and influencing the course of the Cold War.

The U-2 aircraft was developed by Lockheed under the direction of Clarence "Kelly" Johnson. Known as the "Dragon Lady," the U-2 was designed to operate at altitudes above 70,000 feet, far beyond the reach of contemporary Soviet interceptors and surface-to-air missiles. This high-altitude capability allowed the U-2 to conduct reconnaissance missions over Soviet territory, capturing detailed photographs of military installations, missile sites, and other critical infrastructure. These missions were vital for the United States to assess the Soviet Union's military capabilities, particularly regarding its nuclear arsenal.

The U-2 program was a closely guarded secret, operated by the Central Intelligence Agency (CIA). The aircraft's advanced cameras could capture high-resolution images from great heights, providing the U.S. with valuable intelligence. Despite its high-altitude performance, the U-2 had vulnerabilities, including its relatively slow speed and lack of defensive capabilities. Nonetheless, its ability to gather detailed intelligence was considered worth the risk.

The U-2 flights began in 1956, and for several years, they operated without significant incident. However, the Soviet Union was aware of the overflights and was actively working to develop countermeasures.

By 1960, Soviet radar and missile technology had advanced significantly, posing an increasing threat to the U-2 operations. On May 1, 1960, a U-2 piloted by Francis Gary Powers took off from a base in Pakistan on a mission to fly over the Soviet Union and gather intelligence on several key targets.

Powers' flight plan took him over the Ural Mountains, where he was to photograph missile sites and other military installations. However, as the U-2 approached the city of Sverdlovsk, it was detected by Soviet radar. The Soviets launched several surface-to-air missiles (SAMs) to intercept the aircraft. One of the missiles exploded near the U-2, causing severe damage. Despite the plane's altitude, the explosion caused Powers to lose control, and he was forced to bail out. He parachuted to the ground and was promptly captured by Soviet authorities.

The capture of Powers presented a significant dilemma for both the United States and the Soviet Union. Initially, the U.S. government attempted to cover up the incident, claiming that a weather research aircraft had gone off course and was missing. However, Soviet Premier Nikita Khrushchev soon revealed that Powers had been captured alive and had confessed to his espionage mission. The U.S. was caught in a lie, leading to a major international embarrassment.

The fallout from the U-2 Incident was immediate and severe. The incident occurred just days before a scheduled summit in Paris between President Dwight D. Eisenhower, Premier Khrushchev, and other Western leaders. The summit was intended to ease Cold War tensions and discuss critical issues such as arms control and Berlin. However, the U-2 Incident derailed these plans. Khrushchev demanded an apology from Eisenhower and the cessation of U-2 flights over Soviet territory. Eisenhower, while expressing regret for the incident, refused to apologize for the reconnaissance missions, asserting their necessity for national security.

The collapse of the Paris Summit marked a significant setback in U.S.-Soviet relations. The incident underscored the deep mistrust and suspicion that characterized the Cold War, illustrating the lengths to which both superpowers would go to protect their interests and gather intelligence on each other. The U-2 Incident also highlighted the limitations of high-altitude reconnaissance and the growing importance of satellite technology, which would soon become a crucial component of Cold War espionage.

The trial of Francis Gary Powers in Moscow was another critical aspect of the U-2 Incident. Powers was charged with espionage and put on trial in a highly publicized proceeding. The Soviet government used the trial as a propaganda tool, showcasing what it portrayed as American aggression and duplicity. Powers was convicted and sentenced to ten years of imprisonment, including three years of hard labor. However, his time in captivity was relatively short. In February 1962, after nearly two years in prison, Powers was exchanged for Rudolf Abel, a Soviet spy captured by the FBI in the United States, in a dramatic spy swap at the Glienicke Bridge in Berlin.

The U-2 Incident had lasting impacts on various fronts. For the United States, it highlighted the risks and ethical dilemmas of espionage during the Cold War. The incident also exposed the limitations of U-2 flights and accelerated the development and deployment of reconnaissance satellites, which could gather intelligence without the risk of overflights. The U.S. government initiated several intelligence programs, including the Corona program, which launched the first successful reconnaissance satellites, providing a new, safer means of monitoring Soviet activities.

For the Soviet Union, the incident was a propaganda victory, allowing it to portray the U.S. as a violator of international law and an aggressor. It also demonstrated the effectiveness of Soviet air defenses and the vulnerability of U.S. reconnaissance methods. However, the incident also underscored the Soviet Union's own vulnerabilities and the need for improved intelligence-gathering capabilities.

The U-2 Incident also had a profound impact on the personal lives of those involved. Francis Gary Powers returned to the United States to a mixed reception. While some viewed him as a hero, others criticized him for not destroying his aircraft and the intelligence equipment on board before his capture. Powers faced scrutiny and was subjected to multiple investigations, including a Senate hearing, to determine if he had adequately performed his duties. Ultimately, he was exonerated of any wrongdoing and received the Distinguished Flying Cross in 1965. Powers later worked as a test pilot and a helicopter pilot for a television news station until his tragic death in a helicopter crash in 1977.

The legacy of the U-2 Incident continues to be studied and analyzed, offering insights into the complex dynamics of Cold War espionage, international diplomacy, and technological innovation. It serves as a reminder of the high stakes and profound risks involved in intelligence operations and the delicate balance of power during the Cold War. The incident also underscores the importance of transparency, accountability, and ethical considerations in the conduct of espionage and international relations.

The U-2 Incident remains a significant episode in the annals of Cold War history, illustrating the intense competition between the United States and the Soviet Union and the lengths to which both superpowers would go to secure their interests and maintain their security. It is a story of technological innovation, human courage, and the intricate dance of diplomacy and espionage that defined an era of profound geopolitical tension and transformation. As we reflect on the U-2 Incident, we gain a deeper understanding of the complexities of the Cold War and the enduring legacy of this critical period in modern history.

Chapter 8: Operation Ajax: The Coup in Iran

Operation Ajax, also known as the 1953 Iranian coup d'état, represents a pivotal moment in 20th-century history, particularly in the context of U.S. and British intervention in the Middle East. The operation, orchestrated by the American CIA and the British MI6, aimed to overthrow Iran's democratically elected Prime Minister, Mohammad Mossadegh, and reinstall Shah Mohammad Reza Pahlavi as the authoritarian ruler. This covert operation had profound and long-lasting effects on Iran, U.S.-Iran relations, and the geopolitical landscape of the Middle East.

To understand Operation Ajax, it's essential to consider the political and economic climate in Iran in the early 1950s. Iran's significant oil reserves had long been under the control of the British-owned Anglo-Iranian Oil Company (AIOC), which paid Iran a fraction of the profits from its oil production. This arrangement fostered widespread resentment among Iranians, who felt exploited by foreign powers. Mohammad Mossadegh, a prominent nationalist and leader of the National Front, rose to power on a platform of reducing foreign influence and reclaiming control over Iran's resources. In 1951, he successfully pushed for the nationalization of the Iranian oil industry, effectively expelling the AIOC and taking control of the oil fields.

The nationalization of oil was immensely popular in Iran but sparked a severe crisis with Britain. The British government, heavily reliant on Iranian oil, sought to reverse Mossadegh's decision and imposed an international embargo on Iranian oil. This economic blockade severely crippled Iran's economy and heightened internal political tensions. Meanwhile, the British government also turned to the United States for support, emphasizing the strategic importance of

Iran in the Cold War context. British officials argued that a communist takeover in Iran was imminent if Mossadegh remained in power, a claim that resonated with American Cold War anxieties.

Initially, the Truman administration was reluctant to intervene directly in Iran's internal affairs. However, the election of President Dwight D. Eisenhower in 1952 marked a shift in U.S. policy. Eisenhower and his advisors, including Secretary of State John Foster Dulles and his brother, CIA Director Allen Dulles, were staunch anti-communists and more amenable to British arguments. The British, through MI6, presented the coup plan, and with the CIA's involvement, Operation Ajax was conceived. Kermit Roosevelt Jr., a senior CIA officer and grandson of President Theodore Roosevelt, was appointed to lead the operation on the ground in Iran.

The operation's plan involved a combination of political, economic, and propaganda measures designed to undermine Mossadegh's government and create the conditions for a coup. The CIA and MI6 sought to exploit existing divisions within Iranian society and the political elite. They identified key allies, including elements of the Iranian military, conservative clerics, and political figures opposed to Mossadegh. One of the critical figures was General Fazlollah Zahedi, a former officer in the Iranian army with strong anti-Mossadegh sentiments, who was chosen to lead the coup once Mossadegh was deposed.

A significant aspect of Operation Ajax was the propaganda campaign orchestrated by the CIA. Through various means, including bribery, blackmail, and the dissemination of false information, the CIA sought to portray Mossadegh as a corrupt and unstable leader. They also depicted him as a communist sympathizer, despite his nationalist credentials, to exploit Cold War fears. The CIA funded anti-Mossadegh demonstrations, instigated riots, and paid off journalists to write articles critical of Mossadegh. This campaign aimed to create the impression of widespread discontent and unrest, thus justifying the coup as a necessary step to restore order.

The coup began in earnest on August 15, 1953, when elements of the Iranian military, loyal to the Shah and led by Zahedi, attempted to arrest Mossadegh. However, the initial attempt failed, as Mossadegh had been forewarned of the plot. The Shah fled to Rome, fearing for his safety, while Mossadegh's supporters took to the streets to defend his government. For a moment, it seemed that the coup had been thwarted, and Mossadegh's position appeared stronger than ever.

However, the CIA and MI6 did not abandon their efforts. Kermit Roosevelt Jr. stayed in Tehran, coordinating with Zahedi and other coup plotters. Over the next few days, they intensified their efforts, leveraging the existing unrest and continuing their propaganda campaign. On August 19, the situation reached a climax as pro-Shah demonstrators, including organized mobs hired by the CIA, clashed with Mossadegh's supporters. With the assistance of military units loyal to Zahedi, the demonstrators stormed government buildings, and Mossadegh was arrested. The Shah, who had remained in hiding, was invited back to Iran and reinstalled as the ruler.

Operation Ajax was a success from the perspective of the United States and Britain, as it achieved its primary objective of removing Mossadegh from power and reinstating the Shah. However, the coup had profound and far-reaching consequences for Iran and the broader region. The Shah's return marked the beginning of an era of authoritarian rule, characterized by political repression, human rights abuses, and a reliance on a secret police force, the SAVAK, to maintain control. While the Shah embarked on a series of modernization and Westernization programs, his regime's lack of political legitimacy and heavy-handed tactics fueled growing discontent among various segments of Iranian society.

The coup also significantly impacted U.S.-Iran relations. Initially, the Shah maintained close ties with the United States, which provided substantial military and economic aid to his regime. However, the perception that the U.S. had orchestrated the coup to secure its interests, particularly regarding oil, contributed to a deep-seated resentment among many Iranians. This animosity toward foreign intervention and the Shah's regime culminated in the Iranian Revolution of 1979, which saw the overthrow of the Shah and the establishment of the Islamic Republic under Ayatollah Ruhollah Khomeini. The revolution fundamentally altered the geopolitical dynamics of the Middle East and set the stage for a prolonged period of hostility between Iran and the United States.

The legacy of Operation Ajax continues to be a subject of intense debate and reflection. For many Iranians, the coup is a symbol of foreign interference and the betrayal of their democratic aspirations. It serves as a poignant reminder of the complexities and consequences of covert operations and the often-unintended outcomes of foreign intervention. For historians and political analysts, Operation Ajax provides a case study in the dynamics of Cold War geopolitics, the ethics of intelligence operations, and the delicate balance between national interests and international stability.

In recent years, declassified documents and historical research have shed more light on the details of Operation Ajax, providing a clearer understanding of the motivations, strategies, and consequences of the coup. These revelations have prompted discussions about accountability, the long-term impacts of foreign policy decisions, and the lessons that can be learned from past actions. As the world continues to grapple with issues of intervention, sovereignty, and the complexities of international relations, the story of Operation Ajax remains a relevant and cautionary tale.

Operation Ajax's intricate web of political maneuvering, propaganda, and covert action underscores the lengths to which nations will go to protect their interests and influence global events. It highlights the often-hidden forces that shape history and the profound impacts that these actions can have on the lives of individuals and the fate of nations. As we reflect on the events of 1953 and their aftermath, we are reminded of the importance of transparency, accountability, and the pursuit of justice in the conduct of international affairs. The legacy of Operation Ajax continues to resonate, offering valuable insights into the complexities of power, the consequences of intervention, and the enduring quest for self-determination and sovereignty.

Chapter 9: The Venona Project: Decoding Soviet Secrets

The Venona Project, one of the most significant intelligence operations of the 20th century, played a crucial role in uncovering Soviet espionage activities during and after World War II. This top-secret U.S. counterintelligence program, initiated by the Army Signal Intelligence Service (the predecessor of the National Security Agency, or NSA), aimed to decrypt messages sent by Soviet intelligence agencies. The insights gained from the Venona decryptions provided an unprecedented view into Soviet espionage operations and had profound implications for U.S. national security and international relations during the Cold War.

The origins of the Venona Project can be traced back to the early years of World War II, when the United States and the Soviet Union were uneasy allies against the Axis powers. Despite their wartime alliance, there were deep-seated suspicions on both sides. American military and intelligence officials were particularly concerned about the potential for Soviet espionage. In 1943, the Army Signal Intelligence Service began an ambitious effort to intercept and decrypt Soviet communications. This initiative, codenamed Venona, was shrouded in secrecy, with only a handful of top officials aware of its existence.

The task facing the Venona cryptanalysts was formidable. Soviet intelligence agencies, including the KGB (then known as the NKVD) and the GRU (military intelligence), used sophisticated encryption methods to protect their communications. These messages were encrypted using a one-time pad system, considered unbreakable if used correctly. However, due to wartime shortages and other logistical issues, the Soviets sometimes reused their one-time pads, a critical error that created vulnerabilities in their cryptographic security.

The Venona cryptanalysts, led by figures such as Meredith Gardner and Frank Rowlett, painstakingly examined intercepted Soviet messages, searching for patterns and weaknesses. It took years of dedicated effort, but by 1946, they achieved a breakthrough. They managed to decrypt portions of several Soviet messages, revealing a vast and intricate network of Soviet spies operating in the United States. These initial decryptions were just the beginning, and over the following decades, the Venona team would decrypt thousands of Soviet messages, providing invaluable intelligence on Soviet espionage activities.

The decrypted messages, known as Venona intercepts, exposed numerous Soviet espionage operations. One of the most significant revelations was the extent of Soviet infiltration into key U.S. government institutions, including the State Department, the Treasury, and even the atomic bomb project. Among the most infamous spies identified through Venona decrypts were Julius and Ethel Rosenberg, who were implicated in passing atomic secrets to the Soviets. The Venona evidence played a crucial role in their arrest, trial, and eventual execution in 1953.

The Venona decrypts also uncovered the activities of other high-profile Soviet spies, such as Klaus Fuchs, a German-born physicist who worked on the Manhattan Project, and Alger Hiss, a senior State Department official. Fuchs was arrested in 1950 and confessed to passing atomic secrets to the Soviet Union, leading to his conviction and imprisonment. Hiss, who had been accused of espionage by former Soviet spy Whittaker Chambers, was convicted of perjury in 1950 based on the testimony and other evidence, although the Venona decrypts provided further confirmation of his espionage activities.

The Venona Project revealed the extent of Soviet espionage efforts not just in the United States but also in other Allied countries, including Britain, Canada, and Australia. The decrypts showed that the Soviets had penetrated key scientific, military, and political institutions, gathering a wealth of intelligence that helped them develop their atomic bomb much sooner than anticipated. This revelation was a stark reminder of the challenges and dangers posed by Soviet espionage during the early Cold War period.

The existence of the Venona Project remained a closely guarded secret for decades. The intelligence gathered through Venona intercepts was used carefully to avoid revealing the source. Information obtained from the decrypts was often corroborated through other means before being acted upon, and great care was taken to protect the secrecy of the operation. This caution was necessary to ensure that the Soviets remained unaware of the vulnerabilities in their encryption methods, allowing the Venona team to continue their work undetected.

The secrecy surrounding the Venona Project began to lift in the 1990s. In 1995, the U.S. government declassified and released a significant portion of the Venona decrypts, allowing historians and the public to examine this remarkable intelligence achievement. The declassified Venona documents provided new insights into Soviet espionage activities and sparked renewed interest and debate about the extent of Soviet infiltration and the actions taken by the U.S. government in response.

The Venona decrypts have had a profound impact on the historiography of the Cold War and the understanding of Soviet espionage. They provided conclusive evidence of the extensive Soviet espionage network and confirmed the identities of numerous spies, many of whom had been suspected but not definitively proven guilty. This evidence has reshaped the narratives surrounding key historical figures and events, shedding new light on the motivations and actions of individuals involved in espionage.

The revelations from the Venona Project also had significant implications for contemporary politics and society. They reinforced the perception of the Soviet Union as a formidable and aggressive adversary, deeply committed to espionage and subversion. This understanding influenced U.S. policy and public opinion during the Cold War, contributing to the atmosphere of suspicion and vigilance that characterized the era.

Moreover, the Venona decrypts have provided a sobering reminder of the complexities and challenges of counterintelligence work. The meticulous and painstaking efforts of the Venona cryptanalysts demonstrated the critical importance of cryptographic security and the vulnerabilities that can arise from even minor lapses. The project highlighted the necessity of maintaining robust and sophisticated intelligence capabilities to protect national security in an era of intense geopolitical competition.

The legacy of the Venona Project continues to be felt today. The decrypts remain a vital source of information for historians and intelligence professionals, offering valuable lessons on the nature of espionage, the intricacies of cryptography, and the enduring importance of counterintelligence efforts. The Venona documents serve as a testament to the skill, dedication, and ingenuity of the individuals who worked tirelessly to uncover Soviet secrets, providing a clearer understanding of the complex and often hidden dimensions of the Cold War.

Chapter 10: Operation Gladio: NATO's Secret Armies

Operation Gladio is a clandestine operation tied to NATO, with roots tracing back to the Cold War era, characterized by its intricate and covert nature. Initially established in the aftermath of World War II, its primary aim was to prepare for and counter potential Soviet invasions and communist uprisings within Western Europe. This network of secret armies was not merely a contingency plan but an intricate and widespread effort encompassing various European nations, each with its distinct setup yet unified under the broad strategy orchestrated by NATO and Western intelligence agencies, including the CIA and MI6.

The name "Gladio" specifically refers to the Italian branch of these secret armies, derived from the Latin word for a short sword used by Roman gladiators. However, the operation extended far beyond Italy, with parallel structures in countries like Belgium, France, Greece, Germany, and even neutral nations such as Switzerland and Sweden. These stay-behind armies were equipped and trained to perform guerrilla warfare, sabotage, and intelligence gathering should their countries fall under communist control. The operatives often consisted of former soldiers, paramilitary groups, and right-wing extremists who were ideologically opposed to communism and willing to engage in unconventional warfare.

The existence of Operation Gladio and similar networks remained largely unknown to the public until the late 20th century. It was first revealed in 1990 when Italian Prime Minister Giulio Andreotti confirmed the operation's presence in Italy. This disclosure led to a cascade of revelations across Europe, prompting parliamentary inquiries and investigations into the activities and implications of these secret armies. The revelations uncovered not only the strategic intentions behind Gladio but also a series of controversial and often disturbing activities.

One of the most contentious aspects of Operation Gladio involves allegations that these secret armies, or elements within them, engaged in false flag operations and acts of terrorism to manipulate political outcomes. In Italy, for instance, there are claims that Gladio operatives were involved in the so-called "Years of Lead" (Anni di piombo), a period of social and political turmoil marked by widespread terrorism. During this time, Italy experienced numerous bombings, assassinations, and kidnappings, attributed to both far-left and far-right extremist groups. Some researchers and journalists have suggested that certain attacks, ostensibly perpetrated by leftist groups, were actually orchestrated by Gladio operatives or affiliated right-wing extremists to discredit the left and justify repressive measures.

One of the most infamous incidents linked to Gladio is the 1980 Bologna massacre, where a bomb exploded at the Bologna Central Station, killing 85 people and injuring over 200. Initial investigations pointed towards neo-fascist groups, and subsequent inquiries have suggested possible connections to Gladio. While concrete evidence directly linking Gladio to specific terrorist acts remains a subject of debate and speculation, the mere suggestion of such involvement has tainted the operation's legacy and raised profound ethical and legal questions about state-sponsored covert activities.

Beyond Italy, Operation Gladio had significant ramifications in other countries. In Belgium, the revelation of a similar stay-behind network led to public outrage and demands for transparency. Belgian authorities conducted investigations that revealed the existence of clandestine arms caches and secret training programs. Similarly, in France, the discovery of Gladio's operations prompted legislative inquiries and a reevaluation of the country's intelligence practices. In Greece, the network was reportedly involved in the military junta of

1967-1974, illustrating how these secret armies could influence national politics beyond their intended anti-communist mandate.

Switzerland and Sweden, despite their neutrality, also maintained stay-behind networks as part of Gladio. These countries justified their participation by the need to prepare for any potential occupation, whether by the Warsaw Pact or any other hostile force. The Swiss government, for example, acknowledged the existence of P-26, its secret army, and emphasized its role in national defense. However, the broader implications of such clandestine networks in neutral countries remain a point of contention, particularly regarding sovereignty and democratic oversight.

Operation Gladio has had enduring impacts on contemporary understandings of state security, intelligence operations, and international relations. It underscores the lengths to which governments and alliances will go to protect perceived national and ideological interests, even at the cost of transparency and, potentially, the rule of law. The ethical and legal ramifications of such covert operations continue to be relevant in modern debates about intelligence practices, state secrecy, and the balance between security and civil liberties.

The revelations of Gladio have prompted a reassessment of historical narratives regarding the Cold War. They suggest that the conflict was not merely a straightforward geopolitical struggle between the US and the Soviet Union but also involved complex and often murky activities within the Western bloc itself. This includes a willingness to engage in morally ambiguous or outright illegal actions to maintain political stability and counter perceived threats. The uncovering of Gladio has led historians, political scientists, and the public to question the extent to which democratic principles were compromised in the name of anti-communism and the true nature of the threats faced during the Cold War.

Chapter 11: The Israeli Mossad: Capture of Eichmann

The capture of Adolf Eichmann by the Israeli Mossad is a landmark event in the annals of intelligence history, emblematic of determination, meticulous planning, and the pursuit of justice. Eichmann was a high-ranking Nazi official and one of the chief architects of the Holocaust, responsible for the logistics of mass deportation and extermination of Jews during World War II. After the war, he managed to escape capture and evade justice, eventually settling in Argentina under the alias Ricardo Klement. His capture by the Mossad in 1960 was not only a significant achievement in intelligence operations but also a profound moment for Holocaust survivors and the state of Israel.

The operation to capture Eichmann began in earnest in the late 1950s when rumors and fragmented intelligence suggested that he was living in Argentina. Despite the challenges of confirming his identity and exact location, the Israeli government, led by Prime Minister David Ben-Gurion, decided to pursue the matter aggressively. This decision was driven by a deep sense of moral obligation to bring a key perpetrator of the Holocaust to justice, as well as by the symbolic importance of such an act for the nascent state of Israel.

The initial breakthrough came in 1957, when a German-Jewish emigrant named Lothar Hermann, who had settled in Argentina, tipped off Fritz Bauer, a Jewish prosecutor in West Germany, about Eichmann's possible whereabouts. Hermann's daughter, Sylvia, had unwittingly befriended Eichmann's son, Klaus, and gathered enough information to raise suspicions about Klaus's father's true identity. Bauer, aware of the difficulty in pursuing Eichmann through official channels due to geopolitical sensitivities and potential bureaucratic resistance, discreetly passed this intelligence to the Israeli authorities.

Upon receiving Bauer's information, the Mossad, under the leadership of Isser Harel, initiated a covert investigation to verify Eichmann's presence in Argentina. A team of operatives was dispatched to Buenos Aires to conduct surveillance and gather more definitive evidence. This involved painstaking efforts to track Eichmann's movements, observe his routine, and confirm his identity without raising suspicion. The operatives used a variety of tactics, including discreet photography and covert interviews with locals who might have interacted with Eichmann or his family.

Once the Mossad was confident of Eichmann's identity and location, the next phase involved planning and executing his capture. This was an extremely delicate operation, requiring not only precise timing but also careful consideration of legal and diplomatic ramifications. Argentina, at the time, was a haven for many former Nazis and had a government that might not have been sympathetic to an Israeli operation on its soil. Therefore, the mission had to be executed with utmost secrecy to avoid an international incident.

The capture team, consisting of seasoned Mossad agents, flew to Argentina in early May 1960. They set up a safe house and rehearsed their plan meticulously, taking into account various contingencies. The operation's focal point was Eichmann's daily routine of returning home from work by bus, which presented an opportunity for interception. On May 11, 1960, the team put their plan into action. As Eichmann alighted from the bus and walked towards his home on Garibaldi Street in the San Fernando suburb of Buenos Aires, the agents pounced. They wrestled him to the ground, restrained him, and quickly bundled him into a waiting car.

Eichmann was taken to the safe house where he was held for several days while preparations were made to smuggle him out of the country. During his captivity, he was interrogated and eventually admitted his true identity. The next challenge was to transport Eichmann to Israel without arousing the attention of the Argentine authorities or alerting any sympathizers who might attempt to rescue him. The solution came in the form of a covert extraction plan involving a commercial airline.

El Al, Israel's national airline, had a flight scheduled from Buenos Aires to Tel Aviv, ostensibly for the celebration of Israel's Independence Day. Mossad operatives managed to obtain false documents for Eichmann, disguising him as a flight attendant who had fallen ill and needed to be transported back to Israel. On May 20, 1960, Eichmann was sedated, disguised, and flown out of Argentina. The flight landed in Israel on May 22, 1960, where Eichmann was promptly arrested and incarcerated.

The capture of Eichmann was kept secret until May 23, 1960, when Prime Minister Ben-Gurion announced to the Knesset, Israel's parliament, that Eichmann was in Israeli custody and would stand trial for his crimes. This announcement sent shockwaves around the world, eliciting a wide range of reactions from governments, media, and the public. For Holocaust survivors and the Jewish community, it was a moment of profound significance, symbolizing a measure of justice for the unspeakable atrocities committed during the war.

Eichmann's trial, which began on April 11, 1961, in Jerusalem, was one of the most significant legal proceedings of the 20th century. It was not only a trial of a single individual but also a meticulous documentation of the Holocaust itself. Survivors testified, and extensive evidence was presented, shedding light on the bureaucratic and systematic nature of the Nazi genocide. The trial was widely covered by international media, bringing the horrors of the Holocaust to a global audience and reinforcing the importance of memory and justice.

Eichmann was found guilty on multiple counts, including crimes against humanity, war crimes, and crimes against the Jewish people. He was sentenced to death, and on June 1, 1962, he was executed by hanging, the only civil execution ever carried out in Israel. His ashes were scattered at sea, ensuring that no grave could become a site of veneration for neo-Nazis or other extremists.

The successful capture and trial of Adolf Eichmann had profound and lasting impacts. For the state of Israel, it was a powerful affirmation of its commitment to pursuing justice for Holocaust victims and ensuring that perpetrators could not escape accountability. It also served as a stark reminder of the international community's responsibility to combat genocide and uphold human rights.

From an intelligence perspective, the operation showcased the capabilities and resolve of the Mossad, cementing its reputation as one of the world's most effective and resourceful intelligence agencies. The meticulous planning, execution, and successful completion of such a high-risk mission set a benchmark for future operations and demonstrated the critical role of intelligence in achieving national and international security objectives.

The Eichmann operation also had broader implications for international law and the prosecution of war crimes. It underscored the principle that those responsible for atrocities could be held accountable, regardless of time or place. This principle has influenced subsequent efforts to bring war criminals to justice, including the establishment of international tribunals and the International Criminal Court.

In the decades since Eichmann's capture, his trial and its surrounding events have been extensively studied, analyzed, and debated by historians, legal scholars, and ethicists. The operation remains a poignant example of the intersection of justice, memory, and morality in the context of statecraft and intelligence work. It also serves as a powerful narrative of how a determined pursuit of justice, driven by moral imperatives and executed with precision, can leave an indelible mark on history and collective consciousness.

Chapter 12: The Aldrich Ames Spy Scandal

The Aldrich Ames spy scandal stands as one of the most devastating espionage cases in American history, deeply impacting the CIA, U.S. intelligence capabilities, and Cold War dynamics. Aldrich Hazen Ames was a CIA officer who, over a period of nearly a decade, provided critical intelligence to the Soviet Union and later Russia, compromising numerous CIA operations and leading to the deaths of several U.S. sources. The scandal not only exposed significant vulnerabilities within the CIA but also underscored the complexities and dangers of counterintelligence work during a period marked by intense geopolitical rivalry.

Ames's career with the CIA began in 1962 when he joined as a low-level records analyst. Over the years, he held various positions within the agency, slowly climbing the ranks despite a series of professional and personal setbacks. By the mid-1980s, Ames was assigned to the CIA's Soviet-East European division, a position that provided him with access to highly sensitive information about U.S. intelligence operations targeting the Soviet Union.

The turning point in Ames's life came in April 1985 when he decided to approach the Soviet Embassy in Washington, D.C., with an offer to sell classified information. Motivated by financial difficulties and a desire to maintain a lavish lifestyle for himself and his Colombian-born wife, Rosario, Ames agreed to betray his country for substantial financial gain. His initial contact with the Soviets marked the beginning of an extraordinarily damaging espionage operation.

Ames's betrayal had immediate and catastrophic effects. He provided the KGB, the Soviet Union's primary intelligence agency, with a list of every Soviet citizen who was spying for the United States. This included valuable assets such as General Dmitri Polyakov, one of the CIA's top informants within the Soviet military, and Oleg Gordievsky, a senior KGB officer who was spying for the British. As a result, several of these sources were arrested, and many were executed. The loss of these assets severely crippled the CIA's ability to gather intelligence on the Soviet Union during a critical phase of the Cold War.

The financial rewards Ames received in exchange for his treachery were substantial. Over the course of his espionage activities, he received more than $2.7 million from the Soviets, making him the highest-paid spy in U.S. history at that time. Ames and his wife used the money to purchase expensive cars, a large house in Arlington, Virginia, and to finance an extravagant lifestyle far beyond what his CIA salary could afford. The sudden influx of wealth and their conspicuous consumption eventually raised suspicions among Ames's colleagues and within the broader intelligence community.

Despite the mounting losses and growing suspicions, it took several years for the CIA and FBI to identify Ames as the source of the security breaches. Initially, the CIA conducted several internal investigations but failed to pinpoint the cause of the devastating counterintelligence failures. Various other explanations were considered, including the possibility of multiple moles or sophisticated KGB deception operations. During this time, Ames continued to operate with relative impunity, feeding the Soviets a steady stream of invaluable intelligence.

In the early 1990s, the CIA and FBI established a joint mole-hunting task force to resolve the mystery of the compromised operations. This effort involved painstaking analysis of financial records, travel patterns, and behavioral anomalies among CIA personnel. Ames's lavish lifestyle, significant bank deposits, and frequent unauthorized contacts with known Soviet operatives eventually placed him under suspicion. The breakthrough came when the task force uncovered evidence of Ames's unexplained wealth, which correlated with the periods when key intelligence operations had been compromised.

Ames was placed under intense surveillance by the FBI in mid-1993. Investigators monitored his phone calls, intercepted his communications, and followed his movements closely. They also obtained a warrant to search his home, where they found incriminating evidence, including classified documents he had no legitimate reason to possess. The evidence against Ames was overwhelming, and he was arrested on February 21, 1994, along with his wife Rosario, who was charged with conspiracy to commit espionage and money laundering.

The arrest of Ames sent shockwaves through the CIA and the broader intelligence community. His unmasking exposed severe deficiencies in the CIA's internal security and counterintelligence procedures. It also highlighted the ease with which a determined insider could exploit these weaknesses for personal gain, causing immense damage to national security.

Ames and his wife were swiftly prosecuted. Faced with the overwhelming evidence, Ames pled guilty to espionage charges on April 28, 1994, as part of a plea deal to ensure a lighter sentence for his wife. He was sentenced to life in prison without the possibility of parole, while Rosario received a five-year sentence. Ames's conviction and the details of his activities were made public, revealing the extent of his betrayal and the severe consequences for U.S. intelligence.

The fallout from the Ames scandal prompted significant reforms within the CIA and the broader U.S. intelligence community. The agency undertook a comprehensive review of its internal security measures and counterintelligence practices. This led to the implementation of more rigorous background checks, enhanced financial monitoring of personnel, and improved mechanisms for detecting and preventing insider threats. The CIA also strengthened its cooperation with the FBI and other intelligence agencies to improve the sharing of information and coordination of counterintelligence efforts.

The damage caused by Ames's espionage extended beyond the immediate loss of intelligence assets and the compromise of sensitive operations. It had a profound psychological impact on the CIA and its officers, shaking their confidence and trust in the agency's ability to protect its sources and operations. The scandal also strained U.S. relations with its intelligence partners, who became more cautious in their dealings with the CIA, fearing similar breaches of security.

The Ames case serves as a stark reminder of the vulnerabilities inherent in intelligence work and the critical importance of maintaining robust counterintelligence measures. It underscores the need for constant vigilance, thorough vetting of personnel, and the implementation of effective security protocols to protect against insider threats. The lessons learned from the Ames scandal continue to inform the practices and policies of intelligence agencies worldwide, shaping their approach to counterintelligence and internal security in an increasingly complex and interconnected world.

In the broader context of the Cold War and its aftermath, the Ames scandal highlights the enduring challenges of espionage and counterespionage in a world where the stakes are extraordinarily high. The case illustrates how individual motivations, whether financial, ideological, or personal, can intersect with broader geopolitical dynamics to create situations of profound risk and consequence. Ames's betrayal not only compromised U.S. national security but also served as a catalyst for much-needed reforms within the intelligence community, ultimately strengthening its ability to confront future threats.

Chapter 13: The Ultra Project: British Codebreakers

The Ultra Project, one of the most significant intelligence achievements of World War II, involved British codebreakers' efforts to decrypt the encrypted communications of the Axis powers, particularly those of Nazi Germany. The project was centered at Bletchley Park, a Victorian mansion in Buckinghamshire, England, which became the hub of British cryptographic efforts. The successful decryption of the Enigma and later the Lorenz ciphers by the dedicated and brilliant minds at Bletchley Park had a profound impact on the outcome of the war, providing the Allies with critical insights into German military operations and strategic plans.

The roots of the Ultra Project can be traced back to the interwar period when various European countries were working on deciphering encrypted communications. The German Enigma machine, initially developed in the 1920s for commercial purposes, was adopted by the German military in the 1930s and became a cornerstone of their communications strategy. The machine's encryption process was based on a series of rotors and a plugboard, which created a highly complex and seemingly unbreakable code. Each day, the settings of the machine were changed, creating new encryption patterns that were believed to be virtually impossible to crack.

However, early efforts to understand and break the Enigma code began before the outbreak of World War II. In the early 1930s, Polish cryptanalysts, including Marian Rejewski, Jerzy Różycki, and Henryk Zygalski, made significant strides in understanding the Enigma machine's mechanics. They developed methods to reconstruct the wiring of the Enigma rotors and built replicas of the machine. When Germany invaded Poland in 1939, the Polish cryptanalysts shared their findings and techniques with British and French intelligence, providing a crucial foundation for subsequent efforts at Bletchley Park.

At the onset of the war, Bletchley Park was rapidly transformed into a top-secret codebreaking center. The British Government Code and Cypher School (GC&CS) relocated there, bringing together a diverse group of mathematicians, linguists, chess champions, and other intellectuals to tackle the formidable challenge posed by the Enigma. Among these individuals were luminaries such as Alan Turing, Gordon Welchman, Hugh Alexander, and Stuart Milner-Barry, whose contributions were pivotal to the success of the Ultra Project.

Alan Turing, in particular, played a central role in breaking the Enigma code. Turing, a brilliant mathematician and logician, developed the concept of the Bombe, an electromechanical device designed to expedite the process of finding the daily settings of the Enigma machine. The Bombe worked by simulating the Enigma's rotor mechanisms and testing numerous possible configurations to deduce the correct settings. Turing's innovation, along with subsequent refinements and improvements by his colleagues, significantly increased the efficiency of the codebreaking efforts.

The process of breaking Enigma involved not only the technical ingenuity of machines like the Bombe but also the painstaking work of intercepting and analyzing German communications. Radio operators and signal intelligence units intercepted encrypted messages, which were then relayed to Bletchley Park for decryption. The decrypted messages, referred to as "Ultra intelligence," provided invaluable insights into German military strategies, movements, and intentions.

One of the key breakthroughs in the Ultra Project came with the capture of German Enigma machines and codebooks by Allied forces. These captures provided critical information that allowed the codebreakers to better understand the Enigma's daily settings and improve their decryption efforts. Notable incidents included the capture of Enigma materials from U-boat U-559 by the British destroyers HMS Petard and HMS Pakenham, as well as from other German vessels and installations throughout the war.

The intelligence obtained through Ultra had a profound impact on the course of the war. It played a crucial role in several major Allied operations, including the Battle of the Atlantic, where Ultra intelligence helped to counter the U-boat threat and protect vital supply convoys. By decrypting German naval communications, the Allies could reroute convoys away from areas where U-boat wolf packs were operating, significantly reducing losses and ensuring the continued flow of supplies and reinforcements.

Ultra also had a significant impact on the North African campaign, particularly during the battles of El Alamein. By intercepting and decrypting communications between the German High Command and Field Marshal Erwin Rommel, the commander of the Afrika Korps, the Allies gained crucial insights into German troop movements, supply lines, and strategic plans. This intelligence allowed General Bernard Montgomery to outmaneuver Rommel and achieve decisive victories, ultimately leading to the Axis defeat in North Africa.

The Ultra Project's contributions extended to the planning and execution of the D-Day invasion in Normandy. In the lead-up to the invasion, Ultra intelligence provided detailed information about German defenses, troop deployments, and the locations of key military installations along the French coast. This intelligence was instrumental in the meticulous planning of Operation Overlord, the largest amphibious assault in history. On D-Day itself, Ultra intelligence helped the Allies to deceive the Germans about the invasion's timing and location, contributing to the success of the landings and the subsequent liberation of Western Europe.

The impact of Ultra on the Eastern Front was also significant, although less direct. By sharing decrypted intelligence with the Soviet Union, the Allies provided valuable information that helped the Red Army in its operations against the German forces. This cooperation, despite the underlying tensions and mistrust between the Allies and the Soviets, underscored the strategic importance of Ultra intelligence in the broader context of the war.

One of the remarkable aspects of the Ultra Project was the strict secrecy maintained throughout the war and beyond. The existence of Ultra intelligence and the details of the codebreaking efforts at Bletchley Park were closely guarded secrets, known only to a select group of individuals within the British and Allied military and intelligence communities. This secrecy was crucial to ensuring that the Germans remained unaware of the extent to which their communications were being compromised. Any hint that the Enigma code had been broken could have led the Germans to change their encryption methods, potentially nullifying the immense efforts and achievements of the codebreakers.

The success of the Ultra Project was not only a testament to the intellectual prowess and dedication of the individuals at Bletchley Park but also to the collaborative nature of the effort. It involved close cooperation between different branches of the military, intelligence agencies, and Allied nations. The sharing of intelligence and resources, as well as the pooling of diverse talents and expertise, were essential components of the project's success.

After the war, the contributions of the Ultra Project remained classified for several decades. It was only in the 1970s that the existence of Ultra and the codebreaking efforts at Bletchley Park began to be publicly acknowledged. The release of information about the project and the declassification of related documents revealed the full extent of its impact on the war and highlighted the extraordinary achievements of the codebreakers.

The legacy of the Ultra Project extends beyond its immediate contributions to the Allied victory in World War II. It had a lasting influence on the field of cryptography and intelligence, shaping the development of modern computing and information security. Alan

Turing's work on the Bombe and his theoretical contributions to computer science laid the groundwork for the development of modern computers and artificial intelligence. The principles and techniques developed at Bletchley Park continue to inform contemporary cryptographic practices and the ongoing efforts to secure communications in an increasingly digital world.

In addition to its technical and military significance, the Ultra Project also had profound ethical and moral dimensions. The codebreakers at Bletchley Park were acutely aware of the human cost of their work, as their intelligence often directly influenced the outcomes of battles and operations, leading to the loss of lives on both sides. The ethical considerations of their work, the balance between secrecy and the imperative to save lives, and the long-term implications of their actions continue to be subjects of reflection and discussion.

The story of the Ultra Project is a compelling narrative of intellectual brilliance, perseverance, and the strategic importance of intelligence in warfare. It underscores the vital role of cryptography and signals intelligence in modern conflicts and highlights the complexities and challenges of maintaining secrecy and security in the face of determined adversaries. The achievements of the codebreakers at Bletchley Park remain a source of inspiration and a testament to the power of human ingenuity and collaboration in the pursuit of a common goal.

Chapter 14: The Walker Spy Ring: Betrayal in the Navy

The Walker Spy Ring, often described as one of the most damaging espionage cases in American history, involved a network of U.S. Navy personnel and civilian conspirators who, over nearly two decades, provided the Soviet Union with a vast amount of highly classified information. This breach not only compromised national security but also showcased the vulnerabilities in the internal security protocols of the United States Navy. The Walker Spy Ring's activities inflicted significant strategic harm, affecting U.S. military operations and intelligence capabilities during a critical period of the Cold War.

The mastermind behind the espionage ring was John Anthony Walker Jr., a career Navy man who enlisted in 1955 and swiftly rose through the ranks. By 1967, Walker had been promoted to Chief Warrant Officer, a position that granted him access to highly classified information. His motivation for betraying his country was primarily financial; he was struggling with debts and saw espionage as a lucrative way to resolve his financial issues. Walker's betrayal began in 1967 when he walked into the Soviet Embassy in Washington, D.C., and offered his services to the KGB.

Walker's initial offer to the Soviets included a classified document that outlined the capabilities of U.S. naval forces. The KGB recognized the potential value of Walker's access and quickly accepted his offer. Over the next several years, Walker provided the Soviets with a continuous stream of sensitive information, including cryptographic keys, operational plans, and detailed technical manuals. His ability to obtain such information was facilitated by his various assignments on submarines, aircraft carriers, and as a communications specialist.

One of the most significant aspects of Walker's espionage was his access to the cryptographic keys used to secure U.S. Navy communications. These keys allowed the Soviets to decrypt a substantial volume of naval communications, giving them unparalleled insight into U.S. naval operations, strategies, and capabilities. This information was not only valuable for understanding American military movements and plans but also for counterintelligence purposes, as it allowed the Soviets to assess the efficacy of their own espionage activities and adjust their strategies accordingly.

The success of Walker's initial espionage activities led him to expand his network, recruiting several individuals, including his own family members, to assist him. The most prominent recruits were his brother, Arthur Walker, his son, Michael Walker, and a friend, Jerry Whitworth. Each of these individuals played a crucial role in maintaining the flow of classified information to the Soviets.

Arthur Walker, also a retired Navy officer, was recruited in 1980. He provided classified documents he accessed as a defense contractor. His role was to supply John Walker with materials that John could then pass to his Soviet handlers. Arthur's involvement underscored the extent to which John Walker had ingrained himself in a network of individuals with access to sensitive information.

Michael Walker, John's son, was enlisted into the Navy at his father's urging. Michael, serving on the aircraft carrier USS Nimitz, provided his father with classified documents related to naval operations. His position as a Yeoman gave him access to a wide range of sensitive information, which he then passed to his father. Michael's recruitment highlighted the deeply personal and manipulative aspects of John Walker's espionage activities, as he used his own family members to further his betrayal.

Jerry Whitworth, a Navy communications specialist and long-time friend of John Walker, was another key member of the spy ring. Whitworth had access to highly classified communications and cryptographic information, which he passed on to John Walker. Whitworth's involvement added a critical layer to the network, as he provided some of the most sensitive information that the Soviets received.

The Soviet Union highly valued the intelligence provided by the Walker Spy Ring. The information allowed the Soviets to track U.S. naval movements, understand the technological advancements of the U.S. Navy, and develop countermeasures to American strategies. One of the most significant impacts was on the balance of power in naval warfare, as the Soviets were able to anticipate U.S. actions and develop tactics to counter them effectively. The intelligence also had broader strategic implications, influencing the Soviets' overall military planning and geopolitical strategies.

Despite the devastating impact of the Walker Spy Ring, the network remained undetected for years, a testament to both the effectiveness of their operations and the weaknesses in U.S. counterintelligence efforts. It wasn't until the early 1980s that the FBI and Naval Investigative Service (NIS) began to suspect the presence of a mole within the Navy. The investigation gained momentum in 1984 when John Walker's ex-wife, Barbara Walker, approached the FBI. She provided crucial information about John's espionage activities, motivated by both a sense of patriotism and a desire for revenge following their bitter divorce.

Barbara Walker's tip-off initiated an intensive surveillance operation by the FBI, which included wiretaps, physical surveillance, and the monitoring of John Walker's activities. In May 1985, John Walker was observed making a dead drop of classified documents for his Soviet handlers. This evidence was enough for the FBI to move in, and John Walker was arrested on May 20, 1985. Following his arrest, the authorities quickly apprehended the other members of the spy ring.

The subsequent investigation and trials revealed the full extent of the damage caused by the Walker Spy Ring. John Walker, facing overwhelming evidence, cooperated with investigators and provided a detailed account of his espionage activities. His cooperation was part of a plea bargain to secure a lighter sentence for his son, Michael. In 1986, John Walker was sentenced to life imprisonment, and his co-conspirators received various prison terms: Arthur Walker was sentenced to life imprisonment, Jerry Whitworth to 365 years, and Michael Walker to 25 years.

The revelations of the Walker Spy Ring led to significant reforms within the U.S. Navy and the broader intelligence community. The scandal highlighted the need for improved security measures, particularly regarding the handling and protection of classified information. The Navy implemented stricter background checks, enhanced monitoring of personnel with access to sensitive information, and improved cryptographic security measures to prevent similar breaches in the future.

The Walker Spy Ring also had profound implications for U.S. and Soviet relations during the latter stages of the Cold War. The intelligence compromise severely undermined U.S. naval superiority and strategic planning, forcing a reassessment of military capabilities and operational security. It underscored the ongoing espionage struggle between the two superpowers and the critical importance of counterintelligence efforts in maintaining national security.

In the broader context of Cold War espionage, the Walker Spy Ring stands out for its duration, the extent of the compromise, and the profound impact on U.S. military and intelligence operations. The case illustrated the complex motivations behind espionage, including financial gain, personal grievances, and ideological commitments. It also highlighted the challenges of detecting and countering insider threats, even within highly secure and trusted institutions.

The legacy of the Walker Spy Ring continues to influence contemporary intelligence practices and policies. The case serves as a cautionary tale about the vulnerabilities inherent in large, complex organizations and the importance of robust counterintelligence measures. It underscores the need for constant vigilance, rigorous security protocols, and the capacity to adapt to evolving threats in an ever-changing geopolitical landscape.

Chapter 15: Operation Paperclip: Recruiting Nazi Scientists

Operation Paperclip was a secret United States intelligence program in which more than 1,600 German scientists, engineers, and technicians were recruited and brought to America for government employment after the end of World War II. Initiated by the Office of Strategic Services (OSS) and later overseen by its successor, the Central Intelligence Agency (CIA), the program was designed to harness German technological advances and expertise for American military and industrial purposes, while simultaneously denying these resources to the Soviet Union. This controversial operation, which took place from 1945 to 1959, involved figures who had been deeply involved in the Nazi war machine, raising significant ethical and moral questions.

The origins of Operation Paperclip can be traced back to the final years of World War II. As Allied forces advanced into Germany, they discovered a treasure trove of advanced technologies and scientific knowledge that had been developed under the Nazi regime. These included developments in rocketry, jet propulsion, and chemical weapons, among others. Recognizing the strategic value of these technologies, American military and intelligence officials began to devise a plan to acquire them for the United States. This effort was driven by the burgeoning Cold War rivalry with the Soviet Union, which was also actively seeking to exploit German scientific expertise.

One of the most significant areas of interest for the United States was the field of rocketry. During the war, German engineers, led by Wernher von Braun, had developed the V-2 rocket, the world's first long-range guided ballistic missile. The V-2 was a formidable weapon, capable of delivering a one-ton warhead over a distance of 200 miles. Its development marked a significant leap forward in missile technology and posed a serious threat to Allied forces. After the war, capturing the scientists behind this technological marvel became a top priority for American intelligence agencies.

In May 1945, as Germany was collapsing, Wernher von Braun and his team of rocket scientists surrendered to American forces. Recognizing their value, the U.S. Army quickly moved to secure these individuals and their technological knowledge. This initiative, initially called Operation Overcast, was soon renamed Operation Paperclip, after the paperclips used to attach the scientists' personal files to their new records. The operation was formalized by President Harry S. Truman's approval in August 1945, although Truman explicitly stated that no one who had been an active supporter of Nazism or had committed war crimes should be included.

Despite this directive, many of the scientists recruited under Operation Paperclip had troubling pasts. Wernher von Braun, for example, had been a member of the Nazi Party and the SS, and his V-2 rocket program had relied heavily on the labor of concentration camp prisoners, many of whom died under horrific conditions. Other scientists brought to the United States had similarly problematic backgrounds, having been involved in various aspects of the Nazi war effort, including the development of chemical weapons and the implementation of brutal medical experiments.

The moral and ethical implications of Operation Paperclip were profound. The program required the United States to overlook, and in some cases actively conceal, the Nazi affiliations and war crimes of the individuals they were recruiting. This necessitated a significant degree of hypocrisy, as the U.S. had publicly condemned the atrocities committed by the Nazis and had been a driving force behind the Nuremberg Trials, which sought to hold Nazi leaders accountable for their crimes. The decision to recruit these scientists was justified on the grounds of national security and the urgent need to gain a technological edge over the Soviet Union.

The scientists brought to America under Operation Paperclip were dispersed among various military installations and research facilities. Many were assigned to work on projects that would significantly advance American military capabilities. For instance, Wernher von Braun and his team were relocated to Fort Bliss, Texas, where they continued their work on rocket technology. Their efforts culminated in the development of the Redstone missile, which became the foundation for America's intermediate-range ballistic missile program.

One of the most significant legacies of Operation Paperclip was its contribution to the U.S. space program. Von Braun and his team played a pivotal role in the development of the Saturn V rocket, which ultimately enabled the Apollo missions to land American astronauts on the moon. This achievement, celebrated as a triumph of American ingenuity and technological prowess, was in many ways a direct result of the expertise and knowledge gained through Operation Paperclip. The success of the Apollo program cemented the legacy of these former Nazi scientists as key contributors to one of humanity's greatest technological accomplishments.

Beyond rocketry, Operation Paperclip also had a profound impact on other fields. German scientists and engineers contributed to advancements in aeronautics, medicine, and various branches of engineering. For example, Hubertus Strughold, often referred to as the "father of space medicine," made significant contributions to the field of aviation medicine and human spaceflight. However, Strughold's legacy is marred by allegations of his involvement in Nazi medical experiments on concentration camp prisoners, highlighting the ongoing ethical complexities of Operation Paperclip.

The recruitment of these scientists also played a critical role in the early stages of the Cold War. The technological advancements they brought with them helped to establish the United States as a dominant military and technological power, counterbalancing Soviet capabilities. The knowledge and expertise acquired through Operation Paperclip provided the U.S. with a significant advantage in various strategic areas, including missile technology, nuclear weapons development, and electronic warfare.

Despite its successes, Operation Paperclip was shrouded in secrecy and controversy. Many of the details of the program remained classified for decades, and it was not until the late 20th century that the full extent of the operation and the backgrounds of the individuals involved were revealed. This secrecy was driven by the need to protect the reputation of the U.S. government and to avoid public backlash over the recruitment of former Nazis. The revelation of the program's details sparked significant debate and criticism, particularly from Holocaust survivors and human rights advocates who argued that the United States had compromised its moral principles for the sake of expediency.

The legacy of Operation Paperclip is complex and multifaceted. On one hand, the program undeniably contributed to significant technological and scientific advancements that benefited the United States and the world. The contributions of the recruited scientists played a crucial role in the development of key military and space technologies, and their work helped to establish the United States as a leader in these fields. On the other hand, the ethical and moral compromises made to achieve these gains continue to be a source of controversy and debate.

The story of Operation Paperclip also serves as a reminder of the broader ethical dilemmas faced by nations during times of intense geopolitical competition. The decision to recruit former Nazis was driven by the imperative to secure national security and technological superiority in the face of a perceived existential threat from the Soviet Union. This decision reflected a willingness to prioritize strategic interests over moral considerations, a theme that has recurred throughout history in various forms.

In the decades since Operation Paperclip, the ethical considerations surrounding the use of scientific knowledge and expertise obtained through questionable means have continued to resonate. The program has prompted ongoing discussions about the responsibilities of scientists and engineers, the ethical implications of their work, and the importance of maintaining moral integrity in the pursuit of technological and scientific progress.

Chapter 16: The Stuxnet Virus: Cyber Espionage

The Stuxnet virus represents a landmark event in the history of cyber warfare and espionage, showcasing the profound implications of cyber operations on national security and international relations. This sophisticated computer worm, first discovered in 2010, was designed to target and sabotage Iran's nuclear enrichment facilities. Stuxnet's development and deployment are widely attributed to the collaboration between the United States and Israel, marking it as a pioneering effort in state-sponsored cyber-attacks. The virus not only highlighted the vulnerabilities of critical infrastructure to cyber-attacks but also set a precedent for the use of digital weapons in geopolitical conflicts.

Stuxnet was not an ordinary piece of malware. It was a highly sophisticated and complex worm that targeted specific industrial control systems (ICS), particularly those produced by Siemens. These systems are used to manage and control machinery and processes in various industries, including nuclear facilities. The primary target of Stuxnet was the Natanz uranium enrichment plant in Iran, which was central to the country's controversial nuclear program. By targeting the programmable logic controllers (PLCs) that operated the centrifuges used for uranium enrichment, Stuxnet aimed to disrupt and delay Iran's ability to produce weapons-grade uranium.

The complexity and precision of Stuxnet's design were unprecedented. The worm was composed of multiple zero-day exploits—vulnerabilities that were previously unknown and thus had no existing patches—allowing it to spread undetected and penetrate highly secure systems. Stuxnet used four different zero-day exploits, a testament to the resources and expertise behind its development. Once it infiltrated a system, it identified whether the infected machine was connected to the specific Siemens PLCs used at Natanz. If the conditions were met, Stuxnet then altered the PLCs' operation, causing the centrifuges to spin at varying speeds outside their safe operational limits, ultimately damaging or destroying them.

One of the key features of Stuxnet was its ability to operate covertly. It was designed to hide its presence and activities from operators by feeding false data to monitoring systems, making it appear as though everything was functioning normally while the centrifuges were being sabotaged. This level of sophistication required an in-depth understanding of both the target systems and the specific industrial processes they controlled. The designers of Stuxnet also implemented extensive safeguards to ensure the worm would only affect its intended target, minimizing collateral damage to other systems.

The discovery of Stuxnet in June 2010 by the Belarusian security firm VirusBlokAda sent shockwaves through the cybersecurity community. Initially, the malware was identified as a generic worm, but further analysis revealed its true nature and complexity. Cybersecurity experts around the world, including those at Symantec and Kaspersky Lab, began to dissect the code, uncovering its intricate structure and sophisticated capabilities. The realization that Stuxnet was a state-sponsored cyber weapon marked a turning point in the understanding of cyber warfare.

The implications of Stuxnet's deployment were far-reaching. It demonstrated that cyber weapons could be used to achieve strategic military objectives without direct kinetic action, providing a new dimension to modern warfare. The success of Stuxnet in disrupting Iran's nuclear program highlighted the potential of cyber operations to influence geopolitical outcomes. This realization spurred many nations to accelerate the development of their own cyber warfare capabilities, leading to a global cyber arms race.

Stuxnet also exposed the vulnerabilities of critical infrastructure to cyber-attacks. Industrial control systems, which are used to manage everything from power plants to water treatment facilities, were shown to be susceptible to sophisticated malware. This vulnerability has significant implications for national security, as the disruption of such systems could have catastrophic consequences. In response, governments and industries around the world have increased their focus on securing critical infrastructure against cyber threats.

The attribution of Stuxnet to the United States and Israel, though never officially confirmed, is widely accepted based on circumstantial evidence and leaks from various sources. This attribution underscores the growing role of cyber operations in statecraft and the willingness of nations to use cyber tools to achieve strategic goals. The collaboration between the U.S. and Israel in developing Stuxnet reflects the close security partnership between the two countries and their shared interest in curbing Iran's nuclear ambitions.

The ethical and legal implications of Stuxnet's use are complex and controversial. On one hand, proponents argue that Stuxnet achieved its objective of delaying Iran's nuclear program without causing loss of life or significant collateral damage, representing a more precise and less destructive alternative to conventional military strikes. On the other hand, critics contend that the deployment of such a cyber weapon sets a dangerous precedent, potentially legitimizing the use of similar tactics by other nations and non-state actors. The lack of clear international norms and regulations governing the use of cyber weapons further complicates this issue.

The legacy of Stuxnet extends beyond its immediate impact on Iran's nuclear program. It has influenced the development of cybersecurity policies and practices worldwide, prompting governments and industries to reassess their cybersecurity strategies. The incident has also fueled the ongoing debate about the role of offensive cyber operations in national security and the need for international agreements to regulate cyber warfare.

Stuxnet's impact on the field of cybersecurity has been profound. It has driven significant advancements in malware analysis techniques and the development of more robust security measures for industrial control systems. The cybersecurity community has become more vigilant and proactive in identifying and mitigating advanced persistent threats (APTs), which often involve state-sponsored actors. The lessons learned from analyzing Stuxnet have informed the creation of more effective detection and defense mechanisms, enhancing the overall resilience of critical infrastructure against cyber threats.

The geopolitical consequences of Stuxnet continue to resonate today. The use of a cyber weapon to achieve strategic objectives has become a key consideration in the formulation of national security strategies. Nations are increasingly investing in offensive and defensive cyber capabilities, recognizing the potential of cyber operations to influence the balance of power in international relations. The emergence of other state-sponsored cyber-attacks, such as the Russian interference in the 2016 U.S. presidential election and the North Korean WannaCry ransomware attack, highlights the ongoing relevance of cyber warfare in contemporary geopolitics.

Chapter 17: Operation Gold: The Berlin Tunnel

Operation Gold, also known as the Berlin Tunnel, was a clandestine Cold War espionage operation jointly conducted by the United States' Central Intelligence Agency (CIA) and the United Kingdom's Secret Intelligence Service (MI6). The operation, which took place from 1955 to 1956, aimed to tap into Soviet military and intelligence communications in East Berlin by constructing a tunnel to intercept landline communication cables. Despite its ultimate exposure and failure, Operation Gold stands as one of the most audacious and technically ambitious intelligence operations of the Cold War, illustrating the lengths to which intelligence agencies would go to gain a strategic advantage.

The origins of Operation Gold can be traced back to the early 1950s, a period of intense geopolitical tension between the Western powers and the Soviet Union. Berlin, divided into sectors controlled by the Allied powers and the Soviets, was a focal point of Cold War espionage activities. The city's unique status as a divided yet physically connected metropolis made it a prime location for intelligence operations. The idea for the Berlin Tunnel operation emerged from the success of a similar British operation, Operation Silver, which had tapped Soviet communication lines in Vienna. Inspired by this success, the CIA and MI6 sought to replicate the feat in Berlin.

The primary objective of Operation Gold was to tap into Soviet and East German military communications to gather intelligence on their military capabilities, strategic plans, and broader intentions. The project was initiated by William King Harvey, a CIA officer with extensive experience in counterintelligence. Harvey, known for his bold and innovative approach, recognized the potential strategic value of intercepting Soviet communications in Berlin. He proposed constructing a tunnel from the American sector of West Berlin into the Soviet sector of East Berlin to access underground communication cables used by the Soviet military.

The planning and execution of Operation Gold required meticulous preparation and coordination between the CIA and MI6. The project involved extensive technical and logistical challenges, given the need to construct a covert tunnel under one of the most heavily monitored and politically sensitive cities in the world. The construction of the tunnel was carried out in utmost secrecy, with a cover story that it was part of a routine military installation.

Construction of the tunnel began in late 1954. It involved digging a 1,476-foot-long (approximately 450 meters) passage from a specially constructed warehouse in the American sector of Berlin to the target area in the Soviet sector. The tunnel was engineered to avoid detection by Soviet and East German surveillance. To achieve this, the construction team employed various techniques, including soundproofing and vibration damping, to minimize noise and disturbances that could alert the Soviets to the operation. The tunnel was equipped with sophisticated eavesdropping equipment designed to tap into and record communications passing through the underground cables.

One of the key technical challenges was identifying the exact location of the Soviet communication cables. This required detailed reconnaissance and analysis to ensure the tunnel would intersect with the right cables. The cables carried a wealth of information, including military orders, strategic discussions, and intelligence reports, which were invaluable to the Western powers. The intercepted communications would be recorded and analyzed to provide insights into Soviet military capabilities, intentions, and strategies.

Operation Gold's success hinged on maintaining the highest level of secrecy. The project was classified at the highest levels, with only a select group of individuals within the CIA and MI6 aware of its existence. The cover story for the tunnel's construction was carefully crafted to avoid arousing suspicion. The personnel involved in the operation were subject to rigorous security protocols to prevent leaks and maintain operational integrity.

Despite these efforts, Operation Gold was compromised almost from the beginning. Unbeknownst to the CIA and MI6, George Blake, a British intelligence officer who played a key role in planning the operation, was a double agent working for the KGB. Blake had been recruited by the Soviets in the early 1950s and provided them with detailed information about the tunnel project. This allowed the KGB to monitor the operation from its inception, ensuring that the Soviets were aware of every step taken by the Western intelligence agencies.

The Soviets' knowledge of the operation placed them in a unique position. Rather than immediately exposing the tunnel, they decided to allow it to operate for nearly a year, feeding the Americans and British a mix of genuine and deceptive information. This decision enabled the Soviets to gauge the extent of Western intelligence capabilities and intentions while simultaneously managing the flow of information to control what the West learned.

Operation Gold began intercepting Soviet communications in May 1955. For nearly a year, the tunnel successfully recorded thousands of hours of conversations, providing a wealth of intelligence on Soviet military operations and strategic planning. The intercepted communications included discussions on troop movements, military exercises, and political directives. Analysts in Washington and London worked tirelessly to decode and analyze the information, which provided valuable insights into Soviet military capabilities and intentions.

However, in April 1956, the Soviets decided to end the operation. They staged a dramatic discovery of the tunnel, framing it as an act of espionage against the Soviet Union. The exposure of the tunnel was a significant propaganda victory for the Soviets, who used it to denounce

Western espionage activities and reinforce their narrative of Western aggression. The public revelation of the tunnel embarrassed the United States and the United Kingdom, exposing the extent of their covert operations and leading to a diplomatic scandal.

The immediate impact of the tunnel's exposure was a significant blow to Western intelligence efforts in Berlin. The operation's failure highlighted the vulnerabilities of relying on human intelligence and the risks of double agents within intelligence agencies. The exposure also strained diplomatic relations between the Western powers and the Soviet Union, contributing to the broader atmosphere of distrust and hostility that characterized the Cold War.

Despite its failure, Operation Gold had long-term implications for intelligence operations and the conduct of the Cold War. The lessons learned from the operation informed subsequent efforts in signals intelligence and covert operations. The experience underscored the importance of counterintelligence measures to detect and neutralize double agents and emphasized the need for enhanced security protocols in planning and executing covert missions.

The legacy of Operation Gold also includes its contribution to the evolution of technical espionage methods. The operation demonstrated the potential of advanced eavesdropping technology and the value of intercepting communications in gaining strategic intelligence. The technical innovations developed for the tunnel project, such as sophisticated listening devices and soundproofing techniques, influenced future espionage operations and the development of signals intelligence capabilities.

In retrospect, Operation Gold represents a fascinating chapter in the history of Cold War espionage. It exemplifies the audacity and ambition of intelligence agencies during a period of intense geopolitical competition. The operation's mix of technical ingenuity, human intelligence, and strategic deception provides a compelling case study in the complexities and challenges of covert operations.

The story of Operation Gold also serves as a reminder of the ethical and moral dilemmas inherent in espionage. The decision to undertake such a risky and intrusive operation reflected the high stakes of the Cold War and the lengths to which nations would go to gain an advantage. The operation's exposure and the involvement of a double agent highlight the constant interplay between secrecy, deception, and betrayal that defines the world of intelligence.

Chapter 18: The Black Tom Explosion

The Black Tom explosion, which occurred on July 30, 1916, was one of the most significant acts of sabotage on American soil, orchestrated by German agents during World War I. The explosion took place at the Black Tom Island munitions depot in Jersey City, New Jersey, and caused widespread damage, killing several people, injuring hundreds, and resulting in millions of dollars in damage. The event had far-reaching consequences, influencing U.S. public opinion and its eventual entry into World War I, as well as leading to changes in American national security and counterintelligence practices.

The backdrop of the Black Tom explosion was World War I, which had been raging in Europe since 1914. The United States initially maintained a stance of neutrality, with President Woodrow Wilson advocating for peace and non-involvement in the conflict. Despite this official neutrality, American industries were supplying vast quantities of munitions and other war materials to the Allied powers, primarily Britain and France. This support was crucial to the Allied war effort but angered Germany, which sought to disrupt these supplies to weaken its enemies.

German espionage and sabotage activities in the United States were part of a broader campaign to disrupt the supply lines and economic support flowing to the Allies. German agents, under the direction of the German military attaché in Washington, D.C., Franz von Papen, and his associates, engaged in a range of covert operations, including bombing factories, ships, and railways. These activities were facilitated by the relatively lax security measures in place at the time and the ability of German agents to operate relatively freely within the United States.

Black Tom Island was a major munitions depot located in New York Harbor, adjacent to Jersey City. The site was used to store vast quantities of munitions and explosives awaiting shipment to the Allied powers in Europe. On the night of July 29, 1916, the depot was filled with approximately two million pounds of explosives, including TNT and other high explosives. This stockpile represented a significant target for German saboteurs aiming to disrupt the flow of munitions to the Allies.

The exact sequence of events leading to the explosion remains somewhat unclear, but it is believed that German agents infiltrated the depot and planted incendiary devices among the munitions. These devices were designed to ignite and detonate the explosives, causing maximum destruction. At around 2:08 a.m. on July 30, the first explosions occurred, followed by a series of massive blasts that shook the entire region. The explosions were so powerful that they registered on seismographs as far away as Washington, D.C., and were heard as far north as Connecticut and as far south as Maryland.

The immediate impact of the explosion was devastating. The blasts shattered windows across Manhattan, including the stained-glass windows of St. Patrick's Cathedral. Buildings within a half-mile radius were severely damaged, and fragments of metal and debris were thrown over great distances. The nearby Statue of Liberty sustained significant damage, with the torch-bearing arm suffering major structural damage. The explosion also ignited fires that spread rapidly, further exacerbating the destruction.

The human toll of the Black Tom explosion included several deaths and hundreds of injuries. The exact number of casualties remains uncertain, but it is estimated that at least five people were killed, including a police officer, a ten-week-old infant, and several workers at the depot. Many others suffered injuries ranging from cuts and bruises to more severe trauma caused by flying debris and collapsing structures. The financial cost of the explosion was immense, with estimates of the damage ranging from $20 million to $100 million in 1916 dollars (equivalent to hundreds of millions of dollars today).

In the aftermath of the explosion, there was widespread confusion and speculation about its cause. Initial theories ranged from an accident to sabotage, but it quickly became apparent that the scale and nature of the destruction pointed to deliberate action. Investigations were launched by local and federal authorities, including the Bureau of Investigation (the precursor to the FBI) and military intelligence units. These investigations revealed evidence of German involvement, including incendiary devices and the activities of known German agents in the area.

The revelation that the explosion was an act of German sabotage had profound implications for U.S. public opinion and its stance on World War I. Although the United States remained officially neutral at the time, the attack highlighted the vulnerability of American infrastructure and the direct threat posed by German espionage activities. The incident contributed to a growing sentiment among the American public and policymakers that neutrality was becoming increasingly untenable in the face of such aggression.

The Black Tom explosion was a key factor in the eventual decision by the United States to enter World War I. While other incidents, such as the sinking of the Lusitania and the Zimmermann Telegram, also played significant roles, the explosion underscored the direct threat to American security and interests posed by German actions. When the United States declared war on Germany in April 1917, the memory of Black Tom was still fresh in the minds of many Americans, serving as a powerful reminder of the stakes involved.

The legal and diplomatic fallout from the Black Tom explosion was extensive and protracted. The U.S. government pursued claims for damages against Germany, arguing that the sabotage constituted an act of war and seeking compensation for the extensive destruction. The case was complicated by the Treaty of Versailles, which included provisions for war reparations but did not explicitly address acts of sabotage. It was not until 1939, after years of legal battles and negotiations, that Germany agreed to a settlement, paying $50 million in reparations to the United States.

The Black Tom explosion also had a lasting impact on American national security and counterintelligence practices. The incident exposed significant weaknesses in the nation's ability to prevent and respond to acts of sabotage and espionage. In response, the U.S. government implemented a range of measures to enhance security and intelligence capabilities. These included stricter controls on the movement of explosives and other sensitive materials, increased surveillance and monitoring of foreign agents, and the establishment of more robust counterintelligence units.

One of the most significant changes resulting from the Black Tom explosion was the creation of the Bureau of Investigation's General Intelligence Division, which later became the FBI's Counterintelligence Division. This unit was tasked with identifying and neutralizing foreign espionage and sabotage activities within the United States. The lessons learned from the Black Tom incident also informed the development of broader national security policies and practices, laying the groundwork for the modern American intelligence community.

The legacy of the Black Tom explosion extends beyond its immediate impact on World War I and U.S. national security. The event serves as a powerful reminder of the potential for sabotage and espionage to disrupt and damage critical infrastructure, highlighting the importance of vigilance and preparedness in protecting national interests. It also underscores the complex and often covert nature of modern warfare, where acts of sabotage and intelligence operations can have far-reaching consequences.

In the years since the Black Tom explosion, the incident has been the subject of numerous books, documentaries, and scholarly studies, reflecting its enduring significance in American history. The explosion is often cited as one of the earliest and most dramatic examples of state-sponsored terrorism on U.S. soil, predating more well-known incidents such as the bombing of Pearl Harbor and the attacks of September 11, 2001. The story of Black Tom continues to resonate as a cautionary tale about the vulnerabilities of open societies and the persistent threat of sabotage and espionage.

Chapter 19: The CIA's MKUltra: Mind Control Experiments

The CIA's MKUltra program, officially sanctioned in 1953, is one of the most notorious and controversial projects in the history of American intelligence operations. This covert program was designed to explore and develop mind control techniques, leveraging various methods to manipulate mental states and alter brain functions. The ultimate goal was to gain a strategic advantage during the Cold War by discovering ways to control or influence human behavior through psychological and chemical means. Despite being officially terminated in the early 1970s, MKUltra left a lasting legacy of ethical questions, legal battles, and profound mistrust in government activities.

MKUltra was born out of a context of intense geopolitical tension. In the early 1950s, the United States was gripped by fear of Soviet advancements in mind control and brainwashing techniques. Reports of Soviet and Chinese use of such methods during interrogations and their reputed successes in manipulating individuals raised alarms in the U.S. intelligence community. The CIA, under the direction of Director Allen Dulles, sought to counter these threats and even surpass them through its own research into mind control. The project was part of a broader initiative within the CIA known as Project Artichoke, which itself evolved from Project Bluebird, aimed at exploring interrogation and behavioral modification techniques.

MKUltra was spearheaded by Sidney Gottlieb, a chemist who became known as the "Black Sorcerer" and the "Dirty Trickster" due to his central role in overseeing the project. Under Gottlieb's direction, MKUltra encompassed a wide range of experiments involving drugs, hypnosis, sensory deprivation, isolation, verbal and sexual abuse, and other forms of psychological manipulation. One of the most infamous aspects of the program was its use of LSD (lysergic acid diethylamide), a powerful hallucinogen that was still relatively unknown to the public at the time.

The scope of MKUltra was vast, with experiments conducted in universities, hospitals, prisons, and military bases across the United States and Canada. The program operated under extreme secrecy, often without the knowledge or consent of those involved. Many of the subjects were unwitting participants, including patients in psychiatric hospitals, inmates in prisons, and even ordinary citizens who had no idea they were part of a government experiment. This lack of informed consent became one of the most controversial aspects of MKUltra, raising serious ethical and legal concerns.

LSD was at the heart of many MKUltra experiments. The CIA believed that the drug could be used to weaken individuals and force them to confess secrets or comply with commands. Experiments with LSD were conducted on a wide range of subjects, including CIA employees, military personnel, doctors, government agents, prostitutes, mentally ill patients, and members of the general public. The drug was often administered without the subjects' knowledge, leading to unpredictable and sometimes disastrous results. Subjects experienced severe psychological trauma, with some developing long-term mental health issues or committing suicide.

In addition to LSD, MKUltra researchers explored other drugs and chemical substances, including mescaline, heroin, barbiturates, and amphetamines. These substances were used in various combinations to study their effects on mood, perception, cognition, and behavior. The program also investigated methods of inducing amnesia, manipulating memory, and creating altered states of consciousness. Hypnosis was another key area of research, with experiments aimed at understanding how suggestibility could be enhanced and used to control behavior.

One particularly infamous subproject of MKUltra was Operation Midnight Climax, in which the CIA set up safe houses in San Francisco and New York City. These safe houses were equipped with one-way mirrors and recording devices, and they were used to lure unsuspecting individuals, often with the help of prostitutes who were on the CIA's payroll. The subjects were then given LSD and other drugs without their knowledge, and their behavior was observed and recorded. These experiments were ostensibly aimed at studying the effects of drugs in a "natural" setting, but they were marked by serious ethical violations and abuses of power.

The full extent of MKUltra's activities remained hidden from the public for many years. However, in the mid-1970s, a series of investigations brought the program to light. The revelations began with the discovery of documents related to MKUltra during a routine audit of CIA records. These documents, which had survived a 1973 purge of CIA files ordered by then-Director Richard Helms, provided crucial evidence of the program's existence and scope. Subsequent investigations by the U.S. Senate, led by the Church Committee and the Rockefeller Commission, uncovered further details of MKUltra's operations and abuses.

The investigations revealed a program marked by secrecy, deception, and a blatant disregard for ethical standards. The CIA had violated numerous laws and regulations, including those governing the use of human subjects in research. The lack of informed consent, the use of drugs on unwitting subjects, and the psychological and physical harm inflicted on participants all constituted serious ethical breaches. The revelations led to widespread public outrage and a significant erosion of trust in the CIA and the broader intelligence community.

The legal and ethical fallout from MKUltra was substantial. Many of the victims and their families sought justice through the courts, leading to a series of lawsuits against the U.S. government. In some cases, the government settled with plaintiffs, offering compensation for the harm suffered. However, the full extent of the damage caused by MKUltra remains difficult to quantify, given the secrecy surrounding the program and the destruction of many records.

One of the most tragic cases was that of Frank Olson, a CIA scientist who was covertly dosed with LSD in 1953 and subsequently suffered a mental breakdown. Olson fell to his death from a hotel window in New York City, an event that was initially ruled a suicide but later revealed to be more complex, with allegations of foul play and cover-ups. Olson's family pursued legal action against the government, eventually receiving a settlement and an apology from President Gerald Ford, though the full truth behind Olson's death remains a subject of speculation and investigation.

The legacy of MKUltra has had a lasting impact on U.S. intelligence operations and public policy. The program's abuses led to significant changes in the oversight and regulation of research involving human subjects. The National Research Act of 1974 established the National Commission for the Protection of Human Subjects of Biomedical and Behavioral Research, which created guidelines for ethical research practices and the requirement for informed consent. These guidelines have since become the cornerstone of ethical standards in research involving human participants.

MKUltra also left an indelible mark on American culture and public consciousness. The program has been the subject of numerous books, documentaries, and fictional works, reflecting ongoing fascination and horror at the extent of government overreach and the potential for abuse of power. The notion of government mind control and secret experiments has fueled conspiracy theories and skepticism towards government agencies, contributing to a broader climate of mistrust.

In addition to its cultural impact, MKUltra has influenced ongoing debates about the balance between national security and civil liberties. The program's excesses highlighted the dangers of unchecked governmental power and the importance of transparency and accountability in intelligence operations. These lessons remain relevant in contemporary discussions about surveillance, counterterrorism, and the use of technology in intelligence gathering.

Despite the passage of decades, the full scope and impact of MKUltra remain incompletely understood. Many documents related to the program were destroyed, and much of what is known comes from partial records and testimony. Nevertheless, MKUltra stands as a stark reminder of the potential for ethical transgressions in the pursuit of scientific and strategic goals. The program's history underscores the need for vigilance in protecting human rights and ensuring that the quest for knowledge and security does not come at the cost of individual dignity and integrity.

Chapter 20: Operation TPAJAX

Operation TPAJAX, also known as the 1953 Iranian coup d'état, was a covert operation orchestrated by the United States' Central Intelligence Agency (CIA) and the United Kingdom's Secret Intelligence Service (MI6) to overthrow the democratically elected Prime Minister of Iran, Mohammad Mossadegh, and reinstate the Shah of Iran, Mohammad Reza Pahlavi. This operation is one of the most significant examples of Cold War-era interventionism, illustrating the lengths to which Western powers were willing to go to protect their strategic interests, particularly concerning oil resources and regional influence.

The roots of Operation TPAJAX can be traced back to the early 20th century when Iran's vast oil reserves became a critical asset for the British Empire. The Anglo-Persian Oil Company (APOC), later known as the Anglo-Iranian Oil Company (AIOC), controlled Iran's oil industry, securing lucrative contracts that heavily favored British interests while offering minimal benefits to Iran. This imbalance bred resentment among Iranians, who saw their nation's wealth being siphoned off by a foreign power.

In 1951, nationalist sentiment culminated in the election of Mohammad Mossadegh as Prime Minister. Mossadegh, a fervent nationalist, sought to reduce foreign influence and assert greater control over Iran's resources. His most significant move was the nationalization of the AIOC, a bold step that infuriated the British government and threatened their economic interests. Mossadegh's policies were immensely popular in Iran but set him on a collision course with the UK and eventually the US.

The British government, led by Prime Minister Winston Churchill, initially sought to resolve the crisis through economic pressure and diplomatic isolation, imposing an oil embargo on Iran. However, these measures failed to force Mossadegh to reverse his nationalization policy. Frustrated, the British turned to the United States for support, capitalizing on the Cold War context to frame Mossadegh as a potential ally of the Soviet Union, despite his strong nationalist credentials.

The United States, under President Harry S. Truman, initially hesitated to intervene directly in Iran. However, the geopolitical landscape shifted with the election of Dwight D. Eisenhower in 1952. Eisenhower and his administration, particularly Secretary of State John Foster Dulles and his brother Allen Dulles, the Director of Central Intelligence, were more receptive to the British proposal. They viewed Mossadegh's nationalization as a dangerous precedent that could inspire other countries to challenge Western economic dominance, and they feared that political instability in Iran might create an opening for Soviet influence.

Operation TPAJAX, as the coup plan was codenamed by the CIA, was meticulously planned under the supervision of Kermit Roosevelt Jr., a senior CIA officer and grandson of former President Theodore Roosevelt. The operation aimed to depose Mossadegh and strengthen the Shah's power, ensuring that Iran remained a reliable Western ally. The plan involved a multi-faceted strategy of psychological warfare, propaganda, and orchestrating civil unrest to create the impression of widespread dissatisfaction with Mossadegh's government.

One of the key elements of Operation TPAJAX was the use of disinformation and propaganda. The CIA and MI6 funded anti-Mossadegh media campaigns, publishing articles and cartoons in Iranian newspapers that portrayed Mossadegh as a dictator, a communist sympathizer, and a threat to Iran's stability. They also paid off journalists, editors, and influential public figures to spread these messages, creating an atmosphere of distrust and fear.

In addition to propaganda, the operation relied on fomenting street protests and violence. The CIA and MI6 recruited local agents and paid thugs to incite riots, stage demonstrations, and carry out acts of vandalism and intimidation. These actions were designed to create chaos and give the impression that Mossadegh had lost control of the country. The agencies also exploited existing political factions and tensions, playing different groups against each other to further destabilize the government.

A critical turning point came on August 15, 1953, when the first attempt to overthrow Mossadegh, codenamed Operation TPBEDAMN, failed. The Shah, who had initially been hesitant to support the coup, fled to Baghdad and then to Rome, fearing for his safety. Mossadegh, aware of the coup plot, arrested several key military officers involved in the conspiracy. It seemed that the coup had failed, and Mossadegh's position appeared secure.

However, Kermit Roosevelt and his team did not abandon their efforts. They regrouped and intensified their campaign of psychological warfare and disinformation. On August 19, with renewed resolve and additional resources, they launched a second coup attempt. This time, they managed to rally significant portions of the military and security forces, as well as mobilizing mobs through bribery and intimidation. Riots and clashes erupted in Tehran, creating an atmosphere of panic and disorder.

Crucially, the coup plotters secured the support of General Fazlollah Zahedi, a former army officer with strong anti-Mossadegh sentiments. Zahedi was positioned as the leader of the coup and the new prime minister. With Zahedi's backing and the strategic use of force, the coup plotters stormed government buildings, including Mossadegh's residence. After intense fighting, Mossadegh was arrested, and Zahedi took control of the government.

The aftermath of the coup saw the Shah returning to Iran on August 22, 1953, with strong backing from the United States and the United Kingdom. Mossadegh was tried and convicted of treason, receiving a three-year prison sentence followed by house arrest until his death in 1967. The Shah, now firmly reinstated, pursued a policy of consolidation of power, aligning closely with Western interests and cracking down on political dissent.

Operation TPAJAX had profound and long-lasting implications for Iran and the broader Middle East. The immediate outcome was the stabilization of a pro-Western regime in Iran, ensuring the continuation of favorable oil contracts and economic policies that benefitted Western corporations. However, the coup also marked the beginning of a period of autocratic rule by the Shah, characterized by increasing repression and human rights abuses. The Shah's regime, heavily reliant on the support of the United States, grew increasingly unpopular among Iranians, who viewed him as a puppet of Western powers.

The long-term consequences of the coup contributed to significant political and social upheaval in Iran. The resentment towards foreign intervention and the Shah's authoritarian rule fueled nationalist and Islamist opposition movements. These tensions eventually culminated in the Iranian Revolution of 1979, which saw the overthrow of the Shah and the establishment of the Islamic Republic under Ayatollah Ruhollah Khomeini. The revolution marked a dramatic shift in Iran's political landscape and its relations with the West, leading to decades of hostility and confrontation between Iran and the United States.

Operation TPAJAX also had broader implications for U.S. foreign policy and its approach to covert operations. The perceived success of the coup reinforced the belief within the U.S. intelligence community that similar interventions could be effectively used to achieve strategic objectives. This belief influenced subsequent covert operations during the Cold War, including the 1954 coup in Guatemala, the Bay of Pigs invasion in Cuba, and various interventions in Latin America, Africa, and Southeast Asia.

The ethical and moral dimensions of Operation TPAJAX have been the subject of extensive debate and criticism. The operation violated principles of national sovereignty and democratic governance, undermining the legitimacy of Iran's elected government. The use of propaganda, disinformation, and coercion raised serious ethical concerns about the methods employed by the CIA and MI6. The coup also set a troubling precedent for the use of covert action as a tool of foreign policy, contributing to a legacy of mistrust and resentment towards Western interventionism.

In the decades following the coup, the full extent of Operation TPAJAX remained shrouded in secrecy. It was not until the late 1970s and 1980s that declassified documents and historical research shed light on the operation's details and its impact. The release of these documents confirmed the central role of the CIA and MI6 in orchestrating the coup and provided a clearer understanding of the tactics and strategies employed.

In recent years, the legacy of Operation TPAJAX has continued to shape U.S.-Iran relations. The historical memory of the coup remains a potent symbol of foreign interference and betrayal for many Iranians. This legacy has complicated diplomatic efforts and contributed to the deep-seated mistrust that characterizes the relationship between the two countries. The coup is often cited by Iranian leaders and policymakers as a justification for their resistance to U.S. influence and their pursuit of independent foreign and domestic policies.

Chapter 21: The Operation Cyclone: Arming Afghan Rebels

Operation Cyclone was one of the longest and most expensive covert operations conducted by the United States Central Intelligence Agency (CIA). The operation, which spanned from 1979 to 1989, aimed to support and arm Afghan Mujahideen rebels in their fight against the Soviet Union's invasion and subsequent occupation of Afghanistan. This covert action significantly influenced the course of the Cold War, the geopolitical dynamics of South Asia, and the future of Afghanistan itself. The legacy of Operation Cyclone remains controversial due to its profound and often unintended consequences.

The origins of Operation Cyclone can be traced back to the political and strategic landscape of the late 1970s. Afghanistan, a nation with a history of resisting foreign influence, found itself caught in the crosshairs of superpower rivalry. The Soviet Union, seeking to expand its influence and secure its southern borders, supported the Marxist government of the Democratic Republic of Afghanistan, which came to power through a coup in 1978. The new regime, led by the People's Democratic Party of Afghanistan (PDPA), implemented radical socialist reforms that sparked widespread resistance among the traditionally conservative Afghan population.

As opposition to the PDPA grew, the Soviet Union intervened directly in December 1979, sending troops to stabilize the Afghan government and suppress the burgeoning insurgency. This move was seen as a direct threat by the United States, which was already deeply engaged in a global struggle against the spread of communism. The Carter administration, and later the Reagan administration, viewed the Soviet invasion as a critical opportunity to bleed the Soviet Union, drawing it into a costly and protracted conflict akin to the Vietnam War.

Operation Cyclone was officially launched in 1979 under President Jimmy Carter, with National Security Advisor Zbigniew Brzezinski playing a pivotal role in shaping the U.S. response. Brzezinski was a staunch anti-communist who believed that supporting the Afghan Mujahideen was essential to counter Soviet expansionism. The operation was named "Cyclone" to reflect its intended ferocity and impact. Initially, the CIA provided limited financial and logistical support to the Afghan rebels, but the program expanded significantly under President Ronald Reagan.

The primary objective of Operation Cyclone was to supply the Mujahideen with the resources necessary to wage a guerrilla war against the Soviet forces. The CIA funneled money, weapons, and training to various Afghan factions through Pakistan's Inter-Services Intelligence (ISI) agency. The ISI acted as an intermediary, distributing American aid to the Mujahideen while maintaining plausible deniability for the United States. This partnership with Pakistan was crucial, as it provided the rebels with a secure base of operations and logistical support.

The funding for Operation Cyclone grew exponentially over the years. In 1980, the U.S. allocated around $20-30 million to the program. By 1987, this figure had skyrocketed to approximately $630 million annually. In total, it is estimated that the United States spent around $3 billion on Operation Cyclone. This immense financial commitment underscored the importance of the operation to U.S. strategic interests.

One of the most significant aspects of Operation Cyclone was the provision of advanced weaponry to the Mujahideen. Among the various arms supplied, the FIM-92 Stinger missile, a man-portable air-defense system (MANPADS), stood out as a game-changer. Introduced in 1986, the Stinger missile allowed the Mujahideen to effectively target and destroy Soviet helicopters and aircraft, which had previously dominated the battlefield. The introduction of Stinger missiles significantly increased Soviet casualties and aircraft losses, thereby boosting the morale and effectiveness of the Afghan fighters.

The support provided through Operation Cyclone was not limited to weaponry. The CIA also facilitated extensive training programs for the Mujahideen. These training camps, primarily located in Pakistan, focused on guerrilla warfare tactics, sabotage, and the use of modern weaponry. The training was conducted by both CIA operatives and private contractors, as well as Pakistani military personnel. The objective was to create a highly capable and motivated resistance force that could sustain prolonged combat operations against the Soviets.

The composition of the Mujahideen was diverse, encompassing various ethnic groups and ideological factions. This included conservative Islamic groups, nationalist factions, and even more radical Islamist elements. The primary beneficiaries of U.S. support were the conservative and Islamist factions, which were often the most effective and organized. Figures such as Gulbuddin Hekmatyar, Ahmad Shah Massoud, and Jalaluddin Haqqani emerged as prominent leaders within the Mujahideen movement. While these leaders shared a common enemy in the Soviet Union, their visions for Afghanistan's future often diverged significantly.

The impact of Operation Cyclone on the Soviet-Afghan War was profound. The sustained support from the United States, combined with contributions from other countries such as Saudi Arabia and China, enabled the Mujahideen to transform from a disorganized insurgency into a formidable resistance movement. The influx of advanced weaponry and financial resources increased the Mujahideen's operational capabilities, allowing them to launch effective offensives and maintain pressure on Soviet forces.

The war took a heavy toll on both sides. For the Soviet Union, the conflict became a quagmire reminiscent of the United States' experience in Vietnam. The rugged terrain of Afghanistan, coupled with the guerrilla tactics of the Mujahideen, made conventional military operations exceedingly difficult. Soviet forces suffered significant casualties, estimated at around 15,000 soldiers, along with the loss of military equipment and financial resources. The protracted nature of the war strained the Soviet economy and contributed to growing discontent within the Soviet populace and military.

For Afghanistan, the war brought immense suffering and devastation. The conflict resulted in the deaths of an estimated 1 million Afghan civilians, with millions more displaced internally or as refugees in neighboring countries, primarily Pakistan and Iran. The infrastructure of Afghanistan was severely damaged, and the social fabric of the country was torn apart by the violence and upheaval. The Mujahideen, while effective as a resistance force, also engaged in brutal tactics and internal rivalries that further complicated the situation.

Operation Cyclone officially ended with the withdrawal of Soviet forces from Afghanistan in 1989. The Geneva Accords, signed in 1988, facilitated the withdrawal and sought to bring an end to the conflict. However, the accords failed to address the underlying political and social issues within Afghanistan, leading to continued instability and civil war. The departure of the Soviets left a power vacuum that various Mujahideen factions sought to fill, resulting in further conflict and the eventual rise of the Taliban in the mid-1990s.

The legacy of Operation Cyclone is complex and multifaceted. On one hand, the operation achieved its primary objective of weakening Soviet influence and contributing to the eventual collapse of the Soviet Union. The support provided to the Mujahideen played a crucial role in draining Soviet resources and morale, hastening the end of the Cold War. However, the long-term consequences of the operation were far more problematic.

One of the most significant and controversial outcomes of Operation Cyclone was the empowerment of radical Islamist factions within the Mujahideen. Figures such as Osama bin Laden, who later became the leader of al-Qaeda, emerged from the milieu of the Afghan resistance. The extensive network of militant groups and training camps established during the war laid the groundwork for future terrorist organizations. The skills, resources, and ideological fervor cultivated during the conflict would later be directed against the United States and its allies, most notably in the attacks of September 11, 2001.

The aftermath of Operation Cyclone also saw Afghanistan descending into further chaos. The lack of a coherent post-war strategy and the abandonment of Afghanistan by the international community allowed the country to become a breeding ground for extremism and conflict. The civil war that followed the Soviet withdrawal devastated Afghanistan and ultimately led to the rise of the Taliban, a radical Islamist group that imposed a brutal regime on the Afghan people and provided a safe haven for terrorist organizations.

In addition to the geopolitical and security implications, Operation Cyclone had profound humanitarian consequences. The war inflicted immense suffering on the Afghan population, with lasting effects on the country's social and economic development. The destruction of infrastructure, displacement of millions, and loss of human capital set back Afghanistan's progress by decades. The legacy of violence and instability continues to affect the country, as it struggles with ongoing conflict and efforts to rebuild.

Chapter 22: The Church Committee: Exposing CIA Misdeeds

The Church Committee, formally known as the United States Senate Select Committee to Study Governmental Operations with Respect to Intelligence Activities, was established in 1975 to investigate abuses by the CIA, NSA, FBI, and other government agencies. The committee was named after its chairman, Senator Frank Church of Idaho, and its work revealed a staggering array of illegal and unethical activities conducted by U.S. intelligence agencies. The revelations led to significant reforms and a reevaluation of the oversight and accountability mechanisms governing intelligence operations.

The origins of the Church Committee can be traced back to the early 1970s, a period marked by widespread distrust in government institutions. The Vietnam War, the Watergate scandal, and revelations about domestic surveillance and political repression had severely eroded public confidence in the federal government. This atmosphere of skepticism set the stage for a comprehensive examination of intelligence practices.

The impetus for the Church Committee's formation was the publication of the "Family Jewels," a collection of documents compiled by the CIA in response to a request from its then-Director, James Schlesinger. The documents detailed various illegal activities and operations carried out by the CIA over several decades. These included assassination plots against foreign leaders, illegal surveillance of American citizens, and covert actions that violated U.S. laws and international norms. The contents of the "Family Jewels" were leaked to the press, prompting widespread outrage and demands for accountability.

In response to the mounting pressure, the Senate established the Church Committee in January 1975. The committee's mandate was broad, covering all aspects of intelligence operations, including domestic and foreign activities. It was tasked with investigating abuses of power, violations of constitutional rights, and the extent to which intelligence agencies operated outside the bounds of the law. The committee's composition included members from both political parties, reflecting a bipartisan commitment to addressing the issue.

One of the most significant revelations of the Church Committee was the extent of domestic surveillance conducted by the FBI under its COINTELPRO (Counter Intelligence Program). Launched in 1956, COINTELPRO targeted a wide range of groups and individuals deemed subversive or a threat to national security. These included civil rights organizations, anti-war activists, feminist groups, and even prominent figures like Martin Luther King Jr. The program employed various illegal tactics, such as wiretapping, infiltration, disinformation campaigns, and harassment, to disrupt and discredit these groups. The committee's findings revealed a systematic abuse of power by the FBI, highlighting the need for stricter oversight and safeguards to protect civil liberties.

The Church Committee also uncovered numerous covert actions carried out by the CIA, many of which were aimed at influencing political outcomes in other countries. One of the most controversial aspects of the committee's investigation was the exposure of CIA involvement in assassination plots against foreign leaders. Among the most notable targets were Patrice Lumumba of the Congo, Rafael Trujillo of the Dominican Republic, and Fidel Castro of Cuba. These operations, often conducted without presidential authorization or oversight, raised serious ethical and legal questions about the conduct of U.S. foreign policy. The committee's revelations forced a public reckoning with the moral implications of such actions and led to calls for greater transparency and accountability.

Another critical area of investigation was the CIA's MKULTRA program, a series of experiments in mind control and behavioral modification. Initiated in the early 1950s, MKULTRA involved the use of drugs, hypnosis, sensory deprivation, and other methods on unwitting subjects, including U.S. citizens. The aim was to develop techniques for controlling human behavior, ostensibly for use in intelligence and counterintelligence operations. The Church Committee's findings revealed the extent of human rights abuses committed under MKULTRA, including the administration of LSD to unknowing subjects, leading to severe psychological and physical harm. The exposure of these abuses prompted a reevaluation of ethical standards in scientific research and intelligence practices.

The Church Committee also examined the NSA's surveillance activities, which included the monitoring of communications of American citizens without judicial oversight. The committee's investigation revealed that the NSA had engaged in widespread eavesdropping on telephone conversations and other forms of communication, often without warrants or probable cause. This unchecked surveillance posed a significant threat to privacy rights and civil liberties. The committee's findings underscored the need for legal and procedural reforms to ensure that intelligence activities were conducted within the framework of the Constitution.

One of the enduring legacies of the Church Committee was the establishment of permanent oversight mechanisms for intelligence agencies. Prior to the committee's investigation, there was little systematic oversight of the intelligence community, allowing agencies to operate with considerable autonomy and secrecy. The committee's work led to the creation of the Senate Select Committee on Intelligence and the House Permanent Select Committee on Intelligence, both tasked with overseeing the activities of the intelligence community. These bodies were designed to provide continuous and systematic oversight, ensuring that intelligence operations were conducted in accordance with the law and subject to democratic accountability.

The Church Committee also recommended a series of reforms to enhance transparency and accountability within the intelligence community. These included the requirement for intelligence agencies to obtain presidential approval for covert actions, the establishment of clear legal standards for domestic surveillance, and the creation of internal oversight mechanisms within agencies. The committee's recommendations were instrumental in shaping subsequent legislation, such as the Foreign Intelligence Surveillance Act (FISA) of 1978, which established a legal framework for surveillance activities and created the Foreign Intelligence Surveillance Court (FISC) to oversee requests for surveillance warrants.

Despite its significant achievements, the Church Committee faced considerable challenges and criticisms. Some critics argued that the committee's focus on past abuses risked undermining the effectiveness of intelligence agencies and jeopardizing national security. There were concerns that the exposure of covert operations and intelligence methods could compromise ongoing missions and reveal sensitive information to adversaries. Additionally, the political climate of the time, marked by intense partisan divisions, complicated the committee's work and sometimes led to accusations of political bias.

Nevertheless, the Church Committee's legacy remains a vital part of the history of intelligence oversight in the United States. Its investigation brought to light the extent of abuses and misconduct within the intelligence community, prompting a reevaluation of the balance between national security and individual rights. The reforms instituted in the wake of the committee's findings laid the groundwork for a more accountable and transparent intelligence community, although the challenges of oversight and accountability persist.

The Church Committee's work also had a lasting impact on public perceptions of the intelligence community. The revelations of widespread abuses and illegal activities eroded the mystique and secrecy that had long surrounded intelligence agencies. The committee's findings fostered a greater awareness of the potential for abuse of power and the importance of checks and balances in safeguarding democratic values. This legacy continues to inform contemporary debates about the role of intelligence agencies, the limits of government power, and the protection of civil liberties.

Chapter 23: The Dreyfus Affair: A French Scandal

The Dreyfus Affair, a defining episode in French history, began in 1894 when Captain Alfred Dreyfus, a Jewish officer in the French Army, was wrongfully accused and convicted of treason. This scandal revealed deep-seated anti-Semitism, division within French society, and significant flaws in the judicial and military establishments of the Third Republic. Dreyfus was accused of passing military secrets to the German Empire, a charge based on dubious evidence, including a torn-up letter found in a wastebasket at the German Embassy in Paris. This letter, known as the "bordereau," was used to incriminate Dreyfus without substantial proof.

Dreyfus's trial and subsequent conviction were marred by procedural errors and overt prejudice. Despite his protests of innocence, he was found guilty and sentenced to life imprisonment on Devil's Island, a penal colony in French Guiana. The affair might have ended there, with Dreyfus's fate sealed by a corrupt military court, if not for the tireless efforts of his family and supporters who sought to prove his innocence.

The turning point came when Lieutenant Colonel Georges Picquart, the head of French counter-intelligence, discovered evidence suggesting that the real traitor was another officer, Major Ferdinand Walsin Esterhazy. However, Picquart's superiors, more interested in protecting the reputation of the army than in seeking justice, transferred him to a distant post and hushed up his findings. The affair took a dramatic turn when Émile Zola, the famous French writer, published his open letter "J'Accuse...!" in January 1898. Addressed to the President of the Republic, Zola's letter accused the military and government of a cover-up and ignited a fierce public debate. Zola's involvement brought international attention to the case and galvanized the pro-Dreyfus camp, comprising intellectuals, politicians, and ordinary citizens who demanded a retrial.

The Dreyfus Affair polarized French society into two opposing camps: the Dreyfusards, who advocated for justice and the rule of law, and the anti-Dreyfusards, who supported the military's stance and were often motivated by anti-Semitic sentiments. The former saw the affair as a miscarriage of justice that needed to be corrected to uphold the values of the Republic, while the latter viewed any attempt to exonerate Dreyfus as a betrayal of the nation and its army.

Despite mounting evidence of Dreyfus's innocence, the military court acquitted Esterhazy in a sham trial, further inflaming public opinion. The situation grew more contentious with the arrest and trial of Zola for libel, resulting in his conviction and flight to England to avoid imprisonment. However, the relentless campaign by Dreyfus's defenders eventually bore fruit. The affair's critical moment came in 1899, when Dreyfus was brought back to France for a second trial. Although the court once again found him guilty, the sentence was light, and President Émile Loubet granted him a pardon. This was not an admission of innocence but a pragmatic move to quell the growing unrest.

Dreyfus's supporters continued their fight, seeking not just a pardon but full exoneration. It took several more years of legal battles and public advocacy before the truth was officially acknowledged. In 1906, Dreyfus was finally exonerated by the French Supreme Court, reinstated into the army, and promoted to the rank of Major. The Dreyfus Affair had lasting repercussions for France, highlighting the pervasive anti-Semitism within society and the flaws in the judicial system. It also had a profound impact on the French intellectual and political landscape, contributing to the rise of the modern human rights movement and influencing the development of political Zionism, as figures like Theodor Herzl saw the affair as indicative of the deep-rooted anti-Semitism that Jews faced in Europe.

The affair underscored the importance of a free press and the role of public opinion in challenging injustice. It also led to significant reforms in the French military and judicial systems, aimed at preventing such miscarriages of justice in the future. The legacy of the Dreyfus Affair remains relevant today as a cautionary tale about the dangers of prejudice, the importance of due process, and the need for vigilance in protecting individual rights against state abuses.

Chapter 24: The Lavon Affair: Israeli False Flag Operations

The Lavon Affair, also known as Operation Susannah, was a covert Israeli operation in Egypt in the 1950s that ended in scandal and embarrassment for Israel. This incident involved a series of bombings carried out by an Israeli espionage network with the intention of destabilizing Egypt and ruining its relationship with the United States and the United Kingdom. The ultimate goal was to prevent the British from withdrawing their troops from the Suez Canal zone, thus preserving Israel's strategic advantage. The affair was named after Pinhas Lavon, the Israeli Defense Minister at the time, who was believed to have authorized the operation.

In the early 1950s, Egypt, under the leadership of President Gamal Abdel Nasser, was gaining influence in the Arab world and showing increasing hostility toward Israel. At the same time, Britain was planning to withdraw its troops from the Suez Canal zone, a move that Israel feared would strengthen Egypt's position. In response, Israel devised a plan to disrupt the improving relations between Egypt and the Western powers by staging bombings in Egypt and making them appear as though they were carried out by Egyptian nationalists.

Operation Susannah was implemented by a group of Egyptian Jews recruited by Israeli military intelligence. This group, known as Unit 131, was tasked with planting bombs in various civilian targets, including American and British cultural centers, libraries, and other public buildings in Cairo and Alexandria. The plan was for these attacks to create a perception of instability and anti-Western sentiment within Egypt, leading the Western powers to reconsider their support for Nasser's regime.

The operation began in July 1954, with the first bombs planted in Cairo and Alexandria. However, the plan quickly unraveled. On July 2, a bomb prematurely exploded in the pocket of one of the operatives, leading to the capture of several members of the network. Under interrogation, the captured operatives confessed to being part of an Israeli plot, revealing the details of Operation Susannah. The Egyptian authorities arrested the entire network, and their trial received significant international attention. The affair was a major diplomatic embarrassment for Israel, exposing its covert activities and straining its relationships with both the United States and Britain.

The fallout from the Lavon Affair had significant repercussions within Israel as well. Initially, the Israeli government denied any involvement, but the evidence presented by Egypt was overwhelming. A political scandal ensued, leading to a bitter power struggle within the Israeli government. Pinhas Lavon, the Defense Minister, was forced to resign, although he continued to deny authorizing the operation. His resignation marked the beginning of a prolonged period of political turmoil in Israel, with accusations and counter-accusations flying between various political factions.

The affair also led to a series of investigations and trials in Israel. A special ministerial committee was established to investigate the affair, but its findings were inconclusive, leaving many questions unanswered. The scandal remained a contentious issue in Israeli politics for many years, with various individuals and factions using it to settle political scores. In 1960, a new inquiry was launched under the leadership of Haim Cohen, the Attorney General of Israel. This inquiry, known as the Cohen Commission, concluded that Lavon had not authorized the operation, effectively exonerating him. However, the political damage had already been done, and the affair continued to cast a shadow over Israeli politics.

The Lavon Affair also had significant implications for Israeli intelligence operations. The exposure of Unit 131 and the failure of Operation Susannah highlighted the risks and potential consequences of such covert activities. It led to increased scrutiny of Israel's intelligence agencies and their methods, prompting reforms aimed at improving oversight and accountability.

In the broader context of Middle Eastern politics, the Lavon Affair contributed to the growing tension between Israel and its Arab neighbors. The exposure of Israeli covert operations in Egypt fueled anti-Israel sentiment in the Arab world and bolstered Nasser's position as a leader of Arab nationalism. It also reinforced the perception of Israel as a destabilizing force in the region, complicating its diplomatic efforts and relationships with other countries.

Despite the immediate failure and scandal, the Lavon Affair had long-term implications for Israeli strategic thinking. It underscored the importance of intelligence and covert operations in Israel's security doctrine, shaping the development of its intelligence community. The lessons learned from the affair influenced subsequent Israeli operations, emphasizing the need for better planning, execution, and secrecy.

The Lavon Affair also had a lasting impact on the individuals involved. For the operatives who were captured and imprisoned in Egypt, the affair was a personal tragedy. Many of them endured harsh treatment and lengthy sentences, with some remaining in Egyptian prisons for over a decade. Their plight became a rallying point for Israel, with efforts to secure their release continuing for many years.

In retrospect, the Lavon Affair is seen as a cautionary tale about the dangers and complexities of covert operations. It highlights the ethical and strategic dilemmas faced by intelligence agencies and the potential consequences of their actions. The affair serves as a reminder of the delicate balance between national security and diplomatic relations, and the risks inherent in using clandestine methods to achieve political objectives.

Chapter 25: Operation Wrath of God: Mossad's Revenge

Operation Wrath of God, also known as Operation Bayonet, was a covert operation carried out by Israel's intelligence agency, Mossad, in response to the Munich massacre at the 1972 Summer Olympics. This operation aimed to eliminate the individuals responsible for planning and executing the attack, which resulted in the deaths of eleven Israeli athletes and coaches. The operation, which spanned over two decades, involved complex planning, extensive intelligence gathering, and a series of high-profile assassinations across multiple countries.

The Munich massacre was orchestrated by the Palestinian terrorist organization Black September, a faction of the Palestine Liberation Organization (PLO). On September 5, 1972, eight members of Black September infiltrated the Olympic Village in Munich, West Germany, and took eleven members of the Israeli Olympic team hostage. The terrorists demanded the release of 234 Palestinians and non-Arabs jailed in Israel, along with two German left-wing extremists. Negotiations between the German authorities and the terrorists were tense and ultimately unsuccessful. A botched rescue attempt by the German police at Fürstenfeldbruck Air Base led to a firefight, during which all eleven hostages, five of the terrorists, and one German police officer were killed.

The Munich massacre sent shockwaves through Israel and the global community, prompting widespread outrage and calls for justice. The Israeli government, led by Prime Minister Golda Meir, vowed to avenge the murders and authorized Mossad to track down and eliminate those responsible. The operation was named "Wrath of God," reflecting the determination and moral imperative felt by Israel to respond decisively to the atrocity.

Mossad's efforts to bring the perpetrators to justice began with meticulous intelligence gathering. The agency compiled a list of targets, which included key members of Black September and individuals within the broader PLO network who had supported or facilitated the Munich attack. The list included high-profile figures such as Ali Hassan Salameh, the chief of operations for Black September, and Abu Daoud, one of the masterminds behind the massacre. Identifying and locating these individuals required extensive surveillance, the cultivation of informants, and collaboration with other intelligence agencies.

The operation's first major success came on October 16, 1972, when Mossad agents assassinated Wael Zwaiter, a Palestinian poet and translator living in Rome. Zwaiter was believed to be a key figure in Black September, although his exact role in the Munich massacre remains disputed. His death marked the beginning of a relentless campaign that saw Mossad agents carrying out assassinations in various European cities, including Paris, London, Brussels, and Athens.

One of the most notable and controversial incidents during Operation Wrath of God occurred in Lillehammer, Norway, in July 1973. Mossad agents mistakenly identified Ahmed Bouchiki, an innocent Moroccan waiter, as Ali Hassan Salameh. Acting on flawed intelligence, the agents shot and killed Bouchiki in front of his pregnant wife. The botched operation, known as the Lillehammer affair, led to the arrest of several Mossad operatives by Norwegian authorities and sparked a major diplomatic scandal. The incident highlighted the risks and moral ambiguities associated with targeted assassinations and exposed the fallibility of even the most sophisticated intelligence operations.

Despite the setback in Lillehammer, Mossad continued its campaign, adapting its methods and refining its intelligence capabilities. The agency employed a range of tactics, from letter bombs and booby-trapped cars to close-range shootings and coordinated commando raids. Each operation was meticulously planned to minimize collateral damage and ensure the agents' safe extraction. Mossad's operatives, often disguised as tourists, journalists, or businessmen, used forged passports and other false identities to move freely across borders and evade detection.

One of the most significant successes of Operation Wrath of God was the assassination of Ali Hassan Salameh, also known as the "Red Prince." Salameh was a prominent figure within Black September and the PLO, responsible for planning numerous terrorist attacks, including the Munich massacre. After years of evading capture, Salameh was killed in January 1979 in Beirut, Lebanon, when a car bomb planted by Mossad agents detonated as he passed by. His death dealt a significant blow to the PLO and underscored Mossad's persistence and operational capabilities.

Operation Wrath of God also included the establishment of the "Kidon" unit, an elite group within Mossad specializing in targeted assassinations. The unit played a crucial role in executing the operations, combining advanced tradecraft with innovative tactics to eliminate high-value targets. Kidon's operatives were among the most skilled and experienced within Mossad, trained to operate in hostile environments and execute complex missions with precision.

The operation had far-reaching implications beyond the immediate objective of avenging the Munich massacre. It demonstrated Israel's willingness and capability to project power globally and defend its citizens against terrorism. The campaign also served as a deterrent, sending a clear message to terrorist organizations that attacks on Israeli citizens would be met with swift and decisive retaliation. Moreover, Operation Wrath of God contributed to the development of modern counter-terrorism strategies, influencing the tactics and doctrines of intelligence agencies worldwide.

However, the operation was not without controversy and criticism. The ethical and legal implications of targeted assassinations, especially in foreign countries, raised questions about sovereignty, due process, and the rule of law. The deaths of innocent bystanders, as seen in the Lillehammer affair, and the potential for mistaken identity further complicated the moral landscape. Critics argued that the extrajudicial killings undermined international norms and could provoke retaliatory violence, perpetuating a cycle of bloodshed.

In the years following Operation Wrath of God, Israel faced ongoing challenges from terrorist organizations, necessitating continuous adaptation and innovation in its counter-terrorism efforts. The legacy of the operation is complex, marked by both successes and failures, and continues to inform the debate on the effectiveness and morality of targeted killings as a tool of state policy.

Chapter 26: The Operation CHAOS: Spying on Americans

Operation CHAOS was a covert program conducted by the Central Intelligence Agency (CIA) during the 1960s and 1970s aimed at monitoring and infiltrating American political organizations, particularly those involved in the anti-Vietnam War movement. Initiated under the administration of President Lyndon B. Johnson and expanded under President Richard Nixon, the operation represented a significant breach of the CIA's charter, which prohibited it from conducting domestic surveillance. The revelations about Operation CHAOS shocked the American public and led to significant reforms in the oversight of intelligence agencies.

The roots of Operation CHAOS can be traced back to the growing domestic unrest in the United States during the 1960s. As the civil rights movement gained momentum and the opposition to the Vietnam War intensified, the U.S. government became increasingly concerned about the potential influence of foreign powers, particularly the Soviet Union, in fomenting domestic dissent. In response to these concerns, the CIA was tasked with investigating whether the anti-war and civil rights movements were being supported or directed by foreign governments.

Initially, the CIA's involvement in domestic surveillance was relatively limited. However, as protests against the Vietnam War escalated and incidents of civil disobedience became more frequent, President Johnson and his advisors pressured the CIA to expand its activities. This led to the establishment of Operation CHAOS in 1967, with the specific goal of identifying foreign influence within the American anti-war movement. The operation was headed by Richard Ober, a senior CIA officer, and operated under the cover of the agency's Office of Security.

Operation CHAOS was part of a broader counterintelligence effort known as "MH-CHAOS," which included a variety of activities aimed at gathering intelligence on domestic political groups. The program collected information through various means, including surveillance, infiltration, and the use of informants. CIA operatives were embedded within anti-war organizations, student groups, and other political entities to monitor their activities and report back to headquarters. The operation also involved close collaboration with other intelligence and law enforcement agencies, such as the Federal Bureau of Investigation (FBI) and the National Security Agency (NSA).

One of the key aspects of Operation CHAOS was the creation of extensive dossiers on American citizens. These dossiers included detailed personal information, such as political affiliations, social connections, and participation in protests and demonstrations. The CIA amassed thousands of files on individuals and organizations, many of whom were not engaged in any illegal activities but were simply exercising their constitutional rights to free speech and assembly. The sheer scale of the data collection and the invasive nature of the surveillance raised significant concerns about civil liberties and the abuse of government power.

Operation CHAOS expanded significantly under President Nixon, who was particularly paranoid about domestic dissent and perceived threats to his administration. Nixon's obsession with internal security led to the establishment of the White House Special Investigations Unit, also known as the "Plumbers," which was involved in illegal activities such as the break-in at the Democratic National Committee headquarters at the Watergate complex. The same climate of distrust and desire for control that fueled the actions of the Plumbers also influenced the escalation of Operation CHAOS.

Under Nixon, the scope of Operation CHAOS broadened to include not just anti-war activists but also civil rights leaders, journalists, and other perceived political opponents. The operation's reach extended into areas such as mail interception, wiretapping, and the monitoring of overseas communications. The CIA's activities were often conducted with little regard for legal constraints, leading to widespread violations of privacy and civil rights.

The existence of Operation CHAOS remained secret until the early 1970s, when a series of investigative reports and leaks began to expose the extent of domestic surveillance conducted by U.S. intelligence agencies. The New York Times played a crucial role in uncovering the operation, publishing a series of articles in 1974 that detailed the CIA's domestic spying activities. The revelations sparked outrage among the American public and prompted calls for greater oversight and accountability of the intelligence community.

In response to the public outcry, Congress established the Church Committee in 1975, led by Senator Frank Church, to investigate the activities of the CIA, FBI, and other intelligence agencies. The Church Committee's findings were damning, revealing a pattern of abuse and misconduct that extended far beyond Operation CHAOS. The committee's report documented numerous instances of illegal surveillance, harassment, and infiltration of political groups, as well as attempts to influence and disrupt domestic political activities.

The Church Committee's revelations led to significant reforms in the oversight and regulation of the intelligence community. One of the most important outcomes was the establishment of the Foreign Intelligence Surveillance Act (FISA) in 1978, which created a legal framework for the authorization and oversight of electronic surveillance and intelligence gathering on U.S. soil. The FISA court was established to review and approve requests for surveillance warrants, providing a check on the power of intelligence agencies and ensuring that their activities were conducted in accordance with the law.

The aftermath of Operation CHAOS also led to increased scrutiny of the CIA's domestic operations and a reaffirmation of the agency's mandate to focus on foreign intelligence. The CIA's charter was revised to explicitly prohibit it from conducting domestic surveillance, and greater emphasis was placed on transparency and accountability. These reforms were aimed at restoring public trust in the intelligence community and preventing future abuses of power.

Despite these reforms, the legacy of Operation CHAOS continues to resonate in debates about government surveillance and the balance between national security and civil liberties. The operation serves as a cautionary tale about the dangers of unchecked government power and the importance of safeguarding individual rights. It highlights the need for vigilant oversight and the ongoing challenge of ensuring that intelligence agencies operate within the bounds of the law and respect the constitutional rights of citizens.

Chapter 27: The Great Seal Bug

The Great Seal bug, also known as the "Thing," is one of the most fascinating and ingenious devices in the history of espionage. This sophisticated listening device was planted by the Soviet Union inside the U.S. Embassy in Moscow during the Cold War. The story of the Great Seal bug exemplifies the lengths to which intelligence agencies will go to gain an edge over their adversaries and highlights the intricate dance of deception and counterintelligence that characterized the Cold War era.

In 1945, the Soviet Union presented the United States with a beautiful wooden replica of the Great Seal of the United States as a gesture of goodwill. This gift was given by the Soviet Young Pioneers, a communist youth organization, to Averell Harriman, the U.S. Ambassador to the Soviet Union, to commemorate the end of World War II and the strengthening of the Allied relationship. The plaque was displayed with pride in the ambassador's residential study at the Spaso House, the official residence of the U.S. Ambassador in Moscow. However, unbeknownst to the Americans, the plaque contained a cleverly concealed listening device that would allow the Soviets to eavesdrop on confidential conversations for years.

The Great Seal bug was a masterpiece of Soviet ingenuity, designed by Leon Theremin, a Russian inventor best known for creating the theremin, one of the first electronic musical instruments. Theremin's device was revolutionary in that it had no power source or active electronic components that could be easily detected by traditional methods. The bug was a passive resonant cavity microphone, also known as a "passive cavity resonator," which relied on external radio waves to function.

The device worked by having a thin diaphragm connected to a small antenna inside the Great Seal. When sound waves, such as voices, struck the diaphragm, it would cause the antenna to vibrate. These vibrations modulated a radio frequency signal transmitted by a Soviet source outside the embassy. By directing a radio beam at the antenna, the Soviets could pick up the modulated signals and decode the sound waves, allowing them to listen in on conversations taking place in the ambassador's study. The absence of active electronic components made the bug virtually undetectable by the counter-surveillance equipment available at the time.

For seven years, the Great Seal bug transmitted sensitive information to the Soviets without the Americans suspecting a thing. During this period, many high-level discussions and confidential conversations took place in the ambassador's study, providing the Soviets with invaluable intelligence. The device was finally discovered in 1952, not by routine security measures but by sheer luck. The U.S. State Department was conducting a security sweep using a newly developed technique involving microwave technology. When the microwave beam was directed at the Great Seal, it caused an unusual reaction, prompting further investigation.

Upon dismantling the plaque, U.S. security personnel found the hidden device and were stunned by its sophistication. The discovery of the Great Seal bug sent shockwaves through the U.S. intelligence community, leading to a re-evaluation of security protocols and counterintelligence measures. The incident underscored the need for constant vigilance and innovation in the face of evolving espionage threats.

The revelation of the Great Seal bug also had significant diplomatic repercussions. The United States confronted the Soviet Union with evidence of the device, leading to a tense exchange between the two superpowers. The Soviets, of course, denied any wrongdoing, and the incident became another point of contention in the already strained U.S.-Soviet relations. The discovery of the bug highlighted the pervasive atmosphere of distrust and the continuous battle for technological supremacy that characterized the Cold War.

The Great Seal bug's ingenuity lay in its simplicity and effectiveness. It demonstrated the potential of passive surveillance technology and inspired further developments in the field of covert listening devices. The incident also prompted the United States to enhance its own counter-surveillance capabilities, leading to advancements in bug detection and electronic security measures.

The legacy of the Great Seal bug extends beyond its immediate impact on U.S.-Soviet relations. It serves as a stark reminder of the lengths to which nations will go to obtain intelligence and the innovative methods employed by espionage agencies. The device's discovery also fueled an ongoing technological arms race in the field of surveillance and counter-surveillance, driving both superpowers to develop more sophisticated techniques to outsmart each other.

The story of the Great Seal bug also highlights the importance of counterintelligence and the continuous need to adapt to emerging threats. The Americans had placed their trust in the traditional methods of security, which proved inadequate against the novel approach employed by the Soviets. This realization spurred a renewed focus on developing cutting-edge counterintelligence tools and techniques to protect sensitive information.

In the broader context of the Cold War, the Great Seal bug is just one example of the myriad ways in which the United States and the Soviet Union sought to gain an advantage over one another. Espionage was a critical component of this struggle, with both sides deploying an array of tactics and technologies to gather intelligence and protect their own secrets. The constant push and pull of espionage and counterespionage efforts defined much of the Cold War's clandestine conflict, with each side striving to stay one step ahead of the other.

The discovery of the Great Seal bug also had implications for diplomatic security protocols. It led to a heightened awareness of the potential vulnerabilities in seemingly innocuous objects and prompted stricter security measures for gifts and installations within embassies and consulates. This awareness extended to other diplomatic missions worldwide, as nations recognized the need to be vigilant against the possibility of covert surveillance devices being hidden in plain sight.

In the years following the exposure of the Great Seal bug, both the United States and the Soviet Union continued to refine their espionage techniques, leading to a continuous cycle of innovation and counter-innovation. The technological advancements spurred by the need to gain intelligence and protect against surveillance had far-reaching effects, influencing the development of modern-day cybersecurity measures and electronic surveillance methods.

The Great Seal bug incident is also a testament to the enduring relevance of human ingenuity in the field of espionage. Despite the advent of advanced technologies, the basic principles of creativity, innovation, and adaptability remain crucial in the world of intelligence gathering. The Soviet engineers who designed the Great Seal bug demonstrated remarkable ingenuity in leveraging the physics of passive resonant cavity microphones to create a device that was ahead of its time.

Today, the Great Seal bug is remembered as one of the most audacious and effective espionage operations of the Cold War. It stands as a symbol of the clandestine struggle between the United States and the Soviet Union, a struggle that was fought not just on the battlefields but also in the shadows of intelligence operations. The lessons learned from this episode continue to inform modern intelligence practices, emphasizing the importance of vigilance, innovation, and the relentless pursuit of technological advancement in the ever-evolving landscape of espionage.

Chapter 28: Operation Ivy Bells: Wiretapping Underwater

Operation Ivy Bells was a top-secret U.S. Navy and National Security Agency (NSA) mission during the Cold War aimed at tapping Soviet underwater communication cables in the Sea of Okhotsk. This operation, which began in the early 1970s and lasted for more than a decade, represents one of the most audacious and technically challenging espionage efforts in history. It involved sophisticated technology, extraordinary naval capabilities, and a high degree of risk, all undertaken to gather critical intelligence on Soviet naval activities.

The Sea of Okhotsk, a remote and strategically important body of water off the eastern coast of the Soviet Union, was considered by the Soviets to be a secure area for their submarine operations. The Soviet Navy used this sea to test and operate their ballistic missile submarines, which were a key component of their strategic nuclear deterrent. To facilitate secure communication between these submarines and their command centers, the Soviets laid underwater communication cables across the sea floor. These cables were believed to be safe from interception due to their location in Soviet territorial waters, where foreign vessels were not expected to venture.

The United States, keen to gather intelligence on Soviet naval capabilities and strategic plans, saw these cables as a valuable source of information. The challenge was to find a way to tap into these cables without being detected. This task required a combination of advanced technology, specialized submarines, and highly trained personnel. The mission was entrusted to the U.S. Navy's Special Projects Office, which worked closely with the NSA to develop the necessary tools and techniques.

The first step in Operation Ivy Bells was to identify the precise locations of the Soviet communication cables. This involved extensive reconnaissance and mapping efforts, often conducted by U.S. submarines operating covertly in the region. Once the cables were located, the next challenge was to design a device that could be attached to the cables to intercept the communications without damaging them or alerting the Soviets to the operation.

The solution was the development of a sophisticated wiretap device known as a "tap." This device was capable of clamping onto the cable and recording the electromagnetic signals transmitted through it. The tap was designed to be undetectable by the Soviets, with a low-profile and non-intrusive attachment mechanism. It also had to be capable of withstanding the harsh underwater environment, including extreme pressure, cold temperatures, and potential fouling by marine life.

The actual placement of the tap required the use of a specialized submarine, the USS Halibut. The USS Halibut was a unique vessel, originally designed as a guided missile submarine but later converted for special operations. It was equipped with advanced navigation systems, underwater drones, and a diver lockout chamber that allowed divers to exit the submarine while submerged. The Halibut's capabilities made it ideal for the delicate and covert task of placing the wiretap on the Soviet cables.

The mission was executed with meticulous planning and precision. The Halibut would navigate to the target area, relying on its advanced navigation systems to avoid detection by Soviet patrols. Once on site, divers would exit the submarine and carefully attach the wiretap to the cable. The device was designed to be difficult to detect, blending in with the natural surroundings on the sea floor. The tap recorded the communications transmitted through the cable and stored the data in an onboard recording unit, which could later be retrieved by subsequent missions.

One of the most significant aspects of Operation Ivy Bells was the sheer audacity of conducting such a mission in Soviet territorial waters. The Sea of Okhotsk was heavily patrolled by Soviet naval forces, and any detection of U.S. activity could have led to a major international incident. The success of the operation relied on the skill and bravery of the U.S. Navy personnel involved, who operated under the constant threat of discovery and potential capture.

The intelligence gathered from the wiretaps proved to be invaluable. The intercepted communications provided detailed insights into Soviet submarine operations, including the locations, movements, and capabilities of their ballistic missile submarines. This information was crucial for U.S. strategic planners, enabling them to better understand and counter Soviet naval threats. The data also played a significant role in arms control negotiations, as it provided the U.S. with a clearer picture of Soviet strategic capabilities.

Operation Ivy Bells continued successfully for several years, with the taps periodically maintained and upgraded by U.S. submarines. The operation remained a closely guarded secret, known only to a small number of high-ranking officials and intelligence personnel. However, the mission eventually came to an end in the early 1980s, not due to operational failure but because of a significant security breach.

In 1980, Ronald Pelton, a former NSA analyst who was deeply in debt, approached the Soviet Embassy in Washington, D.C., and offered to sell classified information. Pelton, who had knowledge of Operation Ivy Bells, provided the Soviets with detailed information about the mission in exchange for money. His betrayal exposed the operation to the Soviets, who quickly took measures to locate and remove the wiretaps. The discovery of the taps marked the end of Operation Ivy Bells and led to a major counterintelligence investigation by the United States.

Pelton was eventually apprehended by the FBI in 1985 and charged with espionage. His trial revealed the details of Operation Ivy Bells to the public, causing a significant embarrassment for the U.S. intelligence community. Pelton was convicted and sentenced to life imprisonment, highlighting the severe consequences of his actions and the critical importance of safeguarding classified information.

The legacy of Operation Ivy Bells is a testament to the ingenuity, technical prowess, and bravery of the U.S. Navy and intelligence personnel involved. The operation demonstrated the lengths to which nations will go to gain strategic advantages and the critical role of technological innovation in modern espionage. It also underscored the importance of maintaining rigorous security protocols to protect sensitive operations from compromise.

In the broader context of the Cold War, Operation Ivy Bells exemplifies the intense rivalry between the United States and the Soviet Union, a rivalry characterized by a continuous struggle for technological and strategic superiority. The operation's success provided the United States with a significant intelligence edge, contributing to the overall balance of power during a critical period in the Cold War.

The story of Operation Ivy Bells also serves as a reminder of the ethical and legal complexities of espionage. While the operation yielded valuable intelligence, it involved significant risks and operated in a legal gray area, conducting surveillance in the territorial waters of a sovereign nation. The mission's exposure raised questions about the limits of acceptable conduct in intelligence operations and the potential consequences of breaches of trust and security.

Chapter 29: The Cambridge Spy Ring: Soviet Mole at MI6

The Cambridge Spy Ring, also known as the Cambridge Five, represents one of the most significant and damaging intelligence breaches in the history of British espionage. This group of spies, composed of five men recruited at the University of Cambridge in the 1930s, infiltrated the highest levels of the British intelligence and diplomatic services, passing vital information to the Soviet Union for several decades. The members of the Cambridge Spy Ring were Kim Philby, Donald Maclean, Guy Burgess, Anthony Blunt, and John Cairncross. Their espionage activities profoundly affected British and American intelligence operations and strained the relationship between the two allies during the Cold War.

The origins of the Cambridge Spy Ring can be traced back to the ideological climate of the 1930s. During this period, the rise of fascism in Europe and the increasing threat posed by Nazi Germany led many intellectuals and students at Cambridge University to embrace left-wing ideologies. Among them, communism gained a particular appeal as a force against fascism and a pathway to a more just and equitable society. This political environment provided fertile ground for Soviet intelligence agencies, which saw an opportunity to recruit talented and idealistic young individuals who could be groomed for future espionage roles.

The Soviet intelligence agency, then known as the NKVD (later KGB), targeted these promising students with the aim of embedding them within the British establishment. The recruitment of the Cambridge Five was primarily orchestrated by Arnold Deutsch, a Soviet intelligence officer operating under diplomatic cover in London. Deutsch was highly skilled at identifying and persuading young recruits, offering them a chance to fight against fascism and promote socialism on a global scale.

Kim Philby, perhaps the most infamous member of the Cambridge Five, was the first to be recruited. Philby came from a privileged background, his father being a renowned author and explorer. While at Cambridge, Philby became deeply involved in left-wing politics and was introduced to Deutsch through fellow students. Deutsch saw Philby's potential and convinced him to work for the Soviets, emphasizing the moral imperative of combating fascism. Philby's charm, intelligence, and social connections made him an ideal candidate for Soviet espionage.

Donald Maclean and Guy Burgess were recruited shortly after Philby. Maclean, the son of a prominent British diplomat, was a gifted linguist and a fervent communist. Burgess, on the other hand, was a flamboyant and charismatic individual known for his intelligence and connections within the British elite. Both men were deeply committed to the communist cause and readily agreed to serve the Soviet Union. Anthony Blunt, an art historian and a distant relative of the British royal family, was also drawn into the Soviet orbit during his time at Cambridge. John Cairncross, a brilliant scholar with a strong sense of social justice, completed the group.

Upon leaving Cambridge, the members of the spy ring embarked on careers within the British government, military, and intelligence services. Their academic credentials, social connections, and impeccable manners allowed them to rise quickly through the ranks, gaining access to highly sensitive information. Kim Philby joined the Secret Intelligence Service (SIS), commonly known as MI6, where he eventually became the head of counterintelligence for Soviet affairs. Maclean and Burgess entered the Foreign Office, with Maclean serving in key diplomatic posts in Washington, D.C., and Burgess working as a secretary to prominent officials. Blunt took a position within the

British intelligence service MI5 during World War II, and Cairncross worked at Bletchley Park, the British code-breaking center.

Throughout their careers, the Cambridge Five provided the Soviets with a wealth of intelligence. They passed on classified documents, strategic plans, and information about British and American military operations. Their espionage activities were instrumental in informing Soviet strategies during critical moments of the Cold War, including the Berlin Blockade, the Korean War, and the Cuban Missile Crisis. The information supplied by the Cambridge Five enabled the Soviets to anticipate and counter Western actions, significantly enhancing their strategic position.

Kim Philby, in particular, played a pivotal role in Soviet intelligence operations. His position within MI6 allowed him to identify and thwart Western espionage efforts, often leading to the exposure and capture of Western agents operating behind the Iron Curtain. Philby's influence extended to the highest levels of British and American intelligence, where he was trusted and respected by his colleagues. This trust enabled him to manipulate and mislead his superiors, ensuring that his espionage activities remained undetected for many years.

The first major breach in the Cambridge Spy Ring's cover came in 1951, when Donald Maclean's activities aroused suspicion within the British intelligence community. Maclean's increasingly erratic behavior and unexplained absences, coupled with intercepted Soviet communications hinting at a high-level mole within the British government, led to an investigation. Realizing that Maclean was in imminent danger of being exposed, Philby and Burgess orchestrated his escape to the Soviet Union. Burgess, who was also under suspicion, fled with Maclean, creating a scandal that rocked the British establishment.

The defections of Maclean and Burgess sent shockwaves through the British and American intelligence communities, leading to intense scrutiny of their associates. Despite mounting evidence of Philby's involvement, his charm, connections, and persuasive denials allowed him to evade capture. Philby was forced to resign from MI6 but continued to work as a journalist, maintaining his cover while still providing intelligence to the Soviets.

The exposure of the Cambridge Spy Ring continued in 1963, when a Soviet defector, Anatoliy Golitsyn, provided further evidence implicating Philby. This information, combined with growing suspicions within the British intelligence community, finally led to Philby's exposure. In 1963, faced with arrest and interrogation, Philby defected to the Soviet Union, where he lived until his death in 1988. His defection was a major blow to British intelligence, revealing the extent of Soviet infiltration and undermining trust between British and American intelligence agencies.

Anthony Blunt's role in the spy ring was exposed in 1964, following an investigation spurred by the defections of his colleagues. However, Blunt was granted immunity from prosecution in exchange for a full confession, a decision that sparked outrage when it was made public in 1979. Blunt's confession detailed the inner workings of the Cambridge Spy Ring and provided further insights into the extent of Soviet infiltration. John Cairncross's involvement was revealed in the 1970s, rounding out the list of the Cambridge Five.

The legacy of the Cambridge Spy Ring is one of deep betrayal and profound impact on Western intelligence operations. The information passed to the Soviets by the Cambridge Five compromised numerous missions and exposed countless agents, leading to their capture or execution. The ring's activities highlighted the vulnerability of Western intelligence agencies to insider threats and underscored the need for rigorous security measures and counterintelligence efforts.

The Cambridge Spy Ring also had significant implications for the relationship between the United States and the United Kingdom. The exposure of such a high-level penetration of British intelligence led to a period of distrust and tension between the two allies. The United

States, concerned about the potential for further breaches, became more cautious in sharing sensitive information with their British counterparts. This strain was eventually mitigated by mutual efforts to improve security and rebuild trust, but the impact of the Cambridge Spy Ring lingered for years.

The motivations of the Cambridge Five have been the subject of much debate and analysis. While their initial recruitment was driven by ideological commitment to communism and opposition to fascism, the longevity of their espionage activities suggests a complex interplay of factors. Some members, like Philby and Maclean, seemed to genuinely believe in the Soviet cause, while others, like Burgess and Blunt, may have been motivated by a combination of ideology, personal relationships, and a sense of belonging to a covert and exclusive group.

In retrospect, the Cambridge Spy Ring underscores the importance of understanding and addressing the human elements of espionage. Ideological fervor, personal ambition, and social connections all played a role in the recruitment and sustained activities of the Cambridge Five. This recognition has informed modern counterintelligence efforts, which increasingly focus on identifying and mitigating the factors that can lead individuals to betray their country.

The story of the Cambridge Spy Ring also serves as a cautionary tale about the potential for intelligence failures and the challenges of maintaining security in an era of global information exchange. The ring's success in infiltrating the highest levels of British intelligence highlighted the need for continuous vigilance, rigorous vetting processes, and effective counterintelligence strategies. It also emphasized the importance of international cooperation in addressing shared security threats.

Chapter 30: The Rwandan Genocide

The Rwandan Genocide of 1994 stands as one of the most horrific episodes of mass violence in modern history. Over a period of approximately 100 days, an estimated 800,000 to 1,000,000 Tutsis and moderate Hutus were systematically slaughtered by Hutu extremists. This genocide, which took place in the small Central African nation of Rwanda, was marked by extreme brutality and was characterized by the active participation of both civilian and military elements of Rwandan society. In the years following the genocide, significant scrutiny has been placed on the role of international actors, including France, whose intelligence and military support to the Rwandan government at the time has raised critical questions about its involvement and complicity in the events leading up to and during the genocide.

France's involvement in Rwanda dates back to the early 1970s when it began to establish strong ties with the Rwandan government. At that time, Rwanda was led by President Juvénal Habyarimana, who came to power in a coup in 1973. Habyarimana's government was dominated by members of the Hutu ethnic group, which comprised the majority of the Rwandan population. Under Habyarimana's leadership, Rwanda developed close diplomatic and military relations with France, driven by France's broader strategic interests in Africa and its policy of "Françafrique," which sought to maintain French influence over its former colonies and other French-speaking countries in Africa.

Throughout the 1980s and early 1990s, France provided substantial military and financial support to the Habyarimana regime. French military advisers trained the Rwandan armed forces, supplied weapons and military equipment, and provided financial aid that bolstered Habyarimana's government. This support was part of France's broader strategy to counterbalance Anglophone influence in the region, particularly that of Uganda, which had supported the Rwandan

Patriotic Front (RPF), a rebel group composed primarily of Tutsi exiles who had been living in Uganda since the early 1960s.

The RPF, led by Paul Kagame, launched an invasion of Rwanda from Uganda in 1990, seeking to overthrow Habyarimana's government and secure the right of return for Tutsi exiles. The invasion marked the beginning of a protracted civil war that lasted until 1994. During this period, France increased its support to the Rwandan government, providing direct military assistance, including the deployment of French troops under Operation Noroît in 1990 to stabilize the situation and support the Rwandan armed forces against the RPF.

As the conflict continued, tensions between the Hutu and Tutsi populations within Rwanda escalated. The government and its supporters, including extremist Hutu militia groups like the Interahamwe, began to prepare for large-scale violence against the Tutsi population. Propaganda disseminated through state-controlled media, particularly Radio Télévision Libre des Mille Collines (RTLM), dehumanized Tutsis and called for their extermination. During this time, French military and intelligence support to the Habyarimana regime continued unabated.

The critical turning point came on April 6, 1994, when President Habyarimana's plane was shot down near Kigali, killing him and several top officials. The assassination, whose perpetrators remain unidentified, served as the catalyst for the genocide. Within hours of the plane crash, Hutu extremists began a coordinated and systematic campaign of mass murder targeting Tutsis and moderate Hutus. The killing was carried out with ruthless efficiency, involving the military, police, and civilian militias.

French intelligence and military involvement during the genocide itself has been a subject of intense controversy and investigation. Critics argue that France's close relationship with the Habyarimana regime and its continued support to the Rwandan military and government contributed to the conditions that enabled the genocide. French troops, deployed under Operation Amaryllis, were ostensibly in Rwanda to evacuate French nationals and other foreign citizens. However, there have been allegations that French forces also provided assistance to members of the Hutu government and military, facilitating their escape as the RPF advanced and the genocide continued.

In the aftermath of the genocide, France launched Operation Turquoise, a military intervention authorized by the United Nations in June 1994. Operation Turquoise was presented as a humanitarian mission to create a safe zone for refugees and prevent further atrocities. However, the operation has been criticized for its limited effectiveness in stopping the genocide and for providing cover for Hutu perpetrators to flee into neighboring Zaire (now the Democratic Republic of the Congo), where they continued to pose a threat to regional stability.

The Rwandan government, led by the RPF after the genocide, has consistently accused France of complicity in the genocide, alleging that French military and intelligence personnel were aware of and supported the actions of the Hutu extremists. These allegations have been supported by various investigations and reports, including a 2008 report by the Rwandan government, which claimed that French officials, including then-President François Mitterrand, were complicit in the genocide.

French officials have generally denied these allegations, arguing that their actions in Rwanda were intended to maintain stability and protect civilians. Nonetheless, the issue has remained a contentious point in Franco-Rwandan relations, leading to periods of diplomatic tension and calls for further investigation and accountability.

In recent years, there has been a renewed effort to examine France's role in the Rwandan Genocide. In 2019, French President Emmanuel Macron established a commission of historians to investigate France's actions in Rwanda between 1990 and 1994. The commission's report, published in 2021, concluded that France bore "heavy and overwhelming responsibilities" for failing to prevent the genocide. While the report stopped short of accusing France of direct complicity, it highlighted a series of strategic and political errors that contributed to the failure to stop the mass killings.

The revelations of French involvement in the Rwandan Genocide have prompted a broader discussion about the responsibilities of former colonial powers in Africa and the legacy of colonialism. France's actions in Rwanda are seen as part of a larger pattern of intervention and influence in African affairs, often driven by strategic and economic interests rather than humanitarian concerns. This history has led to calls for greater accountability and reparations for the harms inflicted during these interventions.

The impact of the Rwandan Genocide on the survivors and the region cannot be overstated. The genocide left deep scars on Rwandan society, with the loss of a significant portion of the Tutsi population and the widespread trauma experienced by survivors. The aftermath also led to ongoing regional instability, particularly in the Great Lakes region of Africa, where conflicts involving genocidal forces displaced to neighboring countries have continued to pose significant challenges.

Chapter 31: Operation Eavesdrop

Operation Eavesdrop, also known as the FBI's wiretapping of Martin Luther King Jr., represents one of the most notorious and controversial episodes of domestic surveillance in American history. This operation was part of a broader campaign of harassment and surveillance against King, orchestrated by the Federal Bureau of Investigation (FBI) under the leadership of its long-time director, J. Edgar Hoover. The FBI's actions were motivated by a combination of racial prejudice, fears of communist influence, and a desire to discredit and neutralize King's influence in the Civil Rights Movement.

The roots of Operation Eavesdrop can be traced back to the early 1950s, a period marked by intense Cold War paranoia and anti-communist sentiment in the United States. J. Edgar Hoover, who had been the director of the FBI since 1924, was particularly concerned about the potential for communist infiltration of American institutions and movements. The Civil Rights Movement, with its calls for social and political change, was viewed with suspicion by Hoover and his agency. Despite the lack of concrete evidence, the FBI believed that the movement was susceptible to communist influence, a belief that would shape their approach to civil rights leaders, including Martin Luther King Jr.

King first came to the FBI's attention during the Montgomery Bus Boycott of 1955-1956, a pivotal event in the Civil Rights Movement that marked his rise to national prominence. As the leader of the boycott and the newly formed Southern Christian Leadership Conference (SCLC), King became a symbol of nonviolent resistance to racial segregation and injustice. His eloquence, charisma, and growing influence alarmed Hoover, who saw King as a potential threat to the status quo.

Hoover's animosity toward King was further fueled by the Civil Rights Movement's challenge to the systemic racism that was deeply entrenched in American society, including within the FBI itself. The agency's predominantly white leadership and workforce were largely unsympathetic to the goals of the movement and were inclined to view its leaders with suspicion and hostility. This institutional bias was compounded by Hoover's personal animus toward King, whom he viewed as a demagogue and a radical.

The FBI's surveillance of King intensified in 1962 when King hired Stanley Levison, a white attorney and businessman with alleged communist ties, as an advisor. Levison had been involved in various left-wing causes and had previously associated with the Communist Party USA. Although Levison had severed his ties with the party by the time he began working with King, the FBI used his past associations as a pretext to initiate a broader investigation into King's activities.

In 1963, the FBI launched "Operation Eavesdrop," a covert program aimed at monitoring and discrediting King. Under this operation, the FBI sought and obtained authorization from Attorney General Robert F. Kennedy to wiretap King's home and office phones. The official rationale for the wiretaps was to investigate potential communist infiltration of the Civil Rights Movement, but the actual objective was to gather information that could be used to undermine King's credibility and influence.

The wiretaps and other surveillance methods employed by the FBI produced a vast amount of information about King's personal and professional life. Agents monitored his phone calls, bugged his hotel rooms, and followed him during his travels. The surveillance revealed details about King's private affairs, including his extramarital relationships, which the FBI documented meticulously. Hoover believed that exposing King's personal indiscretions would discredit him in the eyes of his supporters and the public, thereby weakening the Civil Rights Movement.

The FBI's campaign against King went beyond mere surveillance. In addition to wiretapping and bugging, the bureau engaged in a range of covert activities designed to harass and intimidate King and his associates. These activities included anonymous letters and phone calls, attempts to sow discord within the SCLC, and efforts to disrupt King's relationships with other civil rights leaders and organizations. One of the most infamous examples of the FBI's harassment was the so-called "suicide letter" sent to King in 1964. The letter, which was accompanied by a tape recording of King's alleged sexual encounters, accused him of moral turpitude and suggested that he should commit suicide to avoid public disgrace. The letter was a thinly veiled attempt to push King to end his life, reflecting the extreme lengths to which the FBI was willing to go to neutralize him.

Despite the FBI's efforts, King continued to lead the Civil Rights Movement and achieve significant successes, including the passage of the Civil Rights Act of 1964 and the Voting Rights Act of 1965. His advocacy for nonviolent resistance and social justice earned him widespread admiration and the Nobel Peace Prize in 1964. However, the relentless surveillance and harassment took a toll on King and his family, contributing to the pressures and stresses he faced as a leader.

The FBI's surveillance of King persisted until his assassination in April 1968. Following his death, the full extent of the bureau's campaign against him began to come to light. In the 1970s, congressional investigations, including the Church Committee hearings, revealed the scope and nature of the FBI's covert operations against King and other civil rights activists. These revelations sparked widespread outrage and led to calls for greater oversight and accountability of intelligence agencies.

The legacy of Operation Eavesdrop and the FBI's campaign against Martin Luther King Jr. has had lasting implications for civil liberties and government surveillance in the United States. The operation exposed the dangers of unchecked government power and the potential for abuse when intelligence agencies are allowed to operate without sufficient oversight. It also highlighted the pervasive influence of racism within government institutions and the extent to which racial prejudice can drive policy decisions and actions.

In response to the abuses uncovered in the 1970s, Congress enacted reforms aimed at increasing transparency and accountability within the intelligence community. These included the establishment of the Foreign Intelligence Surveillance Act (FISA) and the creation of the Senate Select Committee on Intelligence and the House Permanent Select Committee on Intelligence. These measures were intended to provide greater oversight of intelligence activities and to protect the civil liberties of American citizens.

However, the issues raised by Operation Eavesdrop remain relevant today, as debates over government surveillance, privacy, and civil liberties continue to evolve. The balance between national security and individual rights remains a contentious and complex issue, particularly in the context of technological advancements that have expanded the capabilities of intelligence agencies.

The story of Operation Eavesdrop and the FBI's surveillance of Martin Luther King Jr. serves as a powerful reminder of the importance of vigilance in protecting civil liberties and ensuring that government power is exercised responsibly and ethically. It underscores the need for robust oversight mechanisms and a commitment to transparency and accountability in all aspects of government operations.

Martin Luther King Jr.'s legacy as a leader of the Civil Rights Movement and an advocate for social justice endures, and his contributions to the struggle for equality and human rights continue to inspire people around the world. The efforts to undermine and discredit him through surveillance and harassment ultimately failed to diminish his impact or tarnish his memory. Instead, they have become a cautionary tale about the perils of government overreach and the enduring importance of safeguarding the fundamental rights and freedoms that King fought to achieve.

Chapter 32: The Bay of Pigs Invasion: A CIA Disaster

The Bay of Pigs Invasion is a striking example of a failed covert operation that highlighted the perils of intelligence miscalculations and political hubris. In the early 1960s, Cuba, under the leadership of Fidel Castro, was seen by the United States as a significant threat due to its alignment with the Soviet Union during the Cold War. The Eisenhower administration, and later the Kennedy administration, viewed Castro's communist regime as a domino that could potentially influence other Latin American countries to adopt similar political systems, thereby extending Soviet influence in the Western Hemisphere.

The Central Intelligence Agency (CIA) devised a plan to overthrow Castro by training and arming a group of Cuban exiles who would invade Cuba and spark a popular uprising against the communist government. This plan, which came to be known as the Bay of Pigs Invasion, was based on several key assumptions: that the Cuban population would rise up in support of the invaders, that Castro's forces were weak and unprepared, and that the element of surprise would be maintained.

The operation began in earnest on April 15, 1961, with airstrikes intended to destroy Castro's air force. However, these strikes were insufficient and poorly executed, allowing many of Castro's planes to remain operational. Two days later, approximately 1,400 Cuban exiles, trained by the CIA, landed at the Bay of Pigs on Cuba's southern coast. From the outset, the invasion faced numerous challenges. The landing site was a swampy, isolated area, which made it difficult for the invaders to advance. Additionally, the Cuban military, forewarned by various intelligence leaks and suspicious activities, was prepared for the attack.

The invaders, who had expected support from the local population, found little to none. Instead of the anticipated uprising, they faced organized resistance from Castro's forces. Within three days, the invading force was overwhelmed, suffering heavy casualties and many were captured. The lack of effective air support, the isolation of the landing site, and the strong response from Cuban forces turned the invasion into a debacle.

President John F. Kennedy, who had inherited the plan from the Eisenhower administration, faced a difficult decision. He had authorized the operation but opted against deploying American forces to support the exiles, fearing a full-scale war with the Soviet Union. The failure of the Bay of Pigs Invasion was a severe blow to Kennedy's administration, both domestically and internationally. It emboldened Castro, strengthened his ties with the Soviet Union, and humiliated the United States on the world stage.

The aftermath of the invasion had several significant consequences. It solidified Castro's control over Cuba, as he used the failed invasion to galvanize support and crackdown on dissent. The disaster also led to a reevaluation of U.S. intelligence operations and covert activities. The Kennedy administration launched a series of internal investigations to understand what had gone wrong and to prevent similar failures in the future. The incident underscored the dangers of relying on flawed intelligence and the importance of contingency planning in covert operations.

Additionally, the invasion heightened Cold War tensions. It prompted the Soviet Union to increase its military and economic support to Cuba, eventually leading to the Cuban Missile Crisis in October 1962, a confrontation that brought the world perilously close to nuclear war. The failure of the Bay of Pigs Invasion also influenced U.S. foreign policy, leading to a more cautious approach in subsequent interventions and a greater emphasis on intelligence gathering and analysis.

In the broader context of intelligence operations, the Bay of Pigs Invasion serves as a cautionary tale about the complexities of overthrowing a foreign government. It highlighted the need for accurate intelligence, realistic planning, and the understanding that local dynamics and popular support are crucial factors in the success of such operations. The invasion is often studied in military and intelligence circles as an example of what can go wrong when political objectives overshadow practical realities and when decision-makers rely on overly optimistic assumptions.

Chapter 33: The Boston Marathon Bombing

The Boston Marathon Bombing, which occurred on April 15, 2013, stands as a tragic event that highlighted significant shortcomings in the United States' intelligence and counterterrorism apparatus, particularly within the Federal Bureau of Investigation (FBI). This incident, resulting in three deaths and hundreds of injuries, exposed critical gaps in the sharing of information, the evaluation of threats, and the coordination between various intelligence and law enforcement agencies.

The perpetrators of the bombing, Tamerlan and Dzhokhar Tsarnaev, were brothers of Chechen descent who had been living in the United States for several years. Prior to the bombing, Tamerlan had come to the attention of the FBI. In 2011, Russian intelligence services, concerned about his possible connections to extremist groups, alerted the FBI about Tamerlan's potential radicalization. They warned that Tamerlan had become a follower of radical Islam and might be planning to travel to Russia to join unspecified underground groups. The FBI conducted a preliminary investigation, which included interviews with Tamerlan and his family, but found no solid evidence of terrorist activity or intent and subsequently closed the case.

Despite the FBI's initial probe, crucial follow-up actions were not taken. For instance, the FBI did not open a formal investigation, which would have entailed a more thorough and sustained scrutiny. They also failed to inform other pertinent agencies and local law enforcement about Tamerlan's background and the concerns raised by Russian authorities. This lack of communication created a significant blind spot in the monitoring of Tamerlan's activities.

In 2012, Tamerlan traveled to Dagestan and Chechnya, regions known for Islamist insurgency, where he reportedly attempted to join militant groups. However, he returned to the U.S. without being detected or scrutinized further by U.S. intelligence agencies. This trip, which should have raised red flags, did not trigger additional investigation or surveillance upon his return. The lack of coordination and information-sharing between the FBI, the Department of Homeland Security, and other intelligence entities was a critical failure that allowed Tamerlan's activities and potential threats to go unnoticed.

In the months leading up to the bombing, Tamerlan and Dzhokhar Tsarnaev were active online, consuming and interacting with jihadist propaganda. They visited extremist websites and were influenced by radical Islamist ideology. Despite these activities, there was no comprehensive monitoring or intervention by law enforcement agencies. The brothers assembled homemade bombs using pressure cookers, which they filled with shrapnel to maximize casualties. Their actions went undetected by the authorities until the day of the attack.

On April 15, 2013, as the Boston Marathon was in full swing, the Tsarnaev brothers placed their bombs near the finish line. When the devices detonated, the explosions caused immediate chaos and devastation, resulting in the deaths of three spectators and injuries to more than 260 others. The severity and public nature of the attack prompted a massive law enforcement response, leading to one of the largest manhunts in U.S. history.

In the aftermath, the FBI and other agencies faced intense scrutiny for their handling of intelligence prior to the bombing. Congressional hearings and independent reviews highlighted several key failures. One major issue was the inadequate follow-up on the information provided by Russian intelligence. The FBI's limited investigation and the subsequent decision not to share information with local law enforcement were significant oversights. This case underscored the persistent problem of interagency communication and cooperation, which has been a recurring issue in U.S. counterterrorism efforts.

Moreover, the bombing prompted questions about the effectiveness of the Joint Terrorism Task Forces (JTTFs), which are supposed to facilitate collaboration between federal, state, and local agencies. The Boston JTTF's failure to keep local police informed about Tamerlan Tsarnaev exemplified the challenges of ensuring seamless information flow across different jurisdictions and levels of government.

The aftermath of the Boston Marathon Bombing led to several recommendations aimed at improving intelligence operations and counterterrorism measures. These included enhancing the criteria for opening and maintaining investigations into potential threats, improving the mechanisms for sharing intelligence across federal and local agencies, and increasing the oversight of individuals identified as potential risks. Additionally, there was a call for better monitoring of social media and online activities related to radicalization.

Despite these recommendations, the Boston Marathon Bombing remains a stark reminder of the inherent difficulties in preventing domestic terrorism. It highlighted the limitations of the existing intelligence framework and the need for continuous improvements in the detection and prevention of terrorist activities. The bombing also emphasized the importance of vigilance and proactive measures in identifying and mitigating threats before they materialize into tragic events.

Chapter 34: The Assassination of Georgi Markov

The assassination of Georgi Markov is one of the most infamous cases of Cold War espionage and assassination, notable for its methodical execution and the use of a highly unconventional weapon: the poison umbrella. This incident not only highlights the ruthlessness of the Bulgarian secret service, possibly with the assistance of the Soviet KGB, but also underscores the lengths to which intelligence agencies would go to silence dissent during the Cold War era.

Georgi Markov was a Bulgarian dissident writer and journalist who had defected to the West in 1969. Known for his sharp critiques of the Bulgarian government and its leader, Todor Zhivkov, Markov's writings and broadcasts on the BBC World Service, Radio Free Europe, and Deutsche Welle reached a wide audience, much to the chagrin of the Bulgarian authorities. His work exposed the corruption, inefficiency, and brutality of the Communist regime in Bulgaria, making him a prominent enemy of the state.

By the early 1970s, Markov had become a thorn in the side of the Bulgarian government, which viewed his broadcasts as a significant threat to its control over information and public opinion. The regime decided that silencing Markov was imperative. According to various accounts, the Bulgarian secret service, known as the Committee for State Security (DS), sought assistance from the KGB to carry out the assassination. The plan they devised was both elaborate and insidious.

On September 7, 1978, Markov was walking across Waterloo Bridge in London on his way to work at the BBC. As he waited at a bus stop, he felt a sudden sharp pain in the back of his right thigh. When he turned around, he saw a man picking up an umbrella from the ground. The man apologized in a thick foreign accent and quickly crossed the street, disappearing into the crowd. Markov later described the incident to his colleagues, noting the strange nature of the encounter.

By the evening, Markov developed a high fever and was admitted to St. James's Hospital in Balham, London. His condition rapidly deteriorated, and he fell into a coma. Despite the best efforts of the medical staff, Markov died three days later on September 11, 1978. An autopsy revealed a small pellet embedded in his thigh. This pellet, about 1.7 millimeters in diameter, was found to contain tiny holes, which had been filled with the deadly poison ricin. The ricin had been released into Markov's bloodstream, causing his organs to fail.

Ricin is a highly toxic substance derived from castor beans, capable of causing death in minute quantities if ingested, inhaled, or injected. It works by inhibiting protein synthesis in cells, leading to cell death and, ultimately, organ failure. There is no known antidote for ricin poisoning, making it a particularly effective and insidious weapon for assassination.

The use of a modified umbrella to deliver the poison pellet was a masterstroke of clandestine ingenuity. The umbrella had been fitted with a compressed gas mechanism capable of firing the pellet into Markov's leg with enough force to penetrate his skin but without making a noticeable wound. This method allowed the assassin to strike in a crowded public place without drawing attention to himself or the victim.

The investigation into Markov's death quickly pointed to foul play, and suspicion fell on the Bulgarian secret service. The sophistication of the assassination method suggested the involvement of a major intelligence agency, and evidence pointed to the likely assistance of the KGB. British intelligence agencies, including MI5 and Scotland Yard's Special Branch, launched an extensive investigation, but the assassin, believed to be a man named Francesco Gullino (codenamed "Piccadilly"), was never conclusively identified or apprehended. Gullino was an Italian-born Dane who had reportedly been recruited by the Bulgarian secret service, but he remained elusive, and sufficient evidence to bring him to trial was never found.

Markov's assassination sent shockwaves through the international community, highlighting the lengths to which Communist regimes would go to eliminate their critics. It also underscored the complexities and dangers of Cold War espionage, where intelligence agencies employed a wide array of tactics, including sophisticated assassination methods, to achieve their objectives.

The case remained shrouded in mystery for many years, with many details coming to light only after the end of the Cold War. In the 1990s, as Eastern European archives were opened, more information about the Bulgarian secret service and its operations became available. However, many aspects of the case, including the full extent of KGB involvement and the identity of all the operatives involved, remain unclear.

The assassination of Georgi Markov is a chilling reminder of the brutality and reach of Cold War-era intelligence operations. It illustrates how dissidents were targeted and silenced through elaborate and ruthless means. The use of a poison umbrella, a seemingly innocuous everyday object turned into a deadly weapon, captured the imagination of the public and remains a powerful symbol of the clandestine and often lethal nature of espionage activities during that period.

Markov's death also had a significant impact on the perception of the Bulgarian regime and its Soviet allies. It exposed the lengths to which these governments would go to suppress dissent and maintain their grip on power. The incident underscored the risks faced by dissidents and journalists who dared to speak out against authoritarian regimes, highlighting the ongoing struggle for freedom of expression and human rights.

In the years following Markov's assassination, his story has been the subject of numerous books, documentaries, and investigations, keeping the memory of his courage and the circumstances of his death alive in public consciousness. It serves as a stark example of the dangers of state-sponsored violence and the vital importance of protecting those who challenge oppressive regimes.

145

Chapter 35: The Impeachment of Dilma Rousseff

The impeachment of Dilma Rousseff, the 36th president of Brazil, represents one of the most significant and controversial political events in the country's recent history. While the primary charges against Rousseff were related to budgetary manipulation, the backdrop of this political upheaval includes allegations and suspicions of espionage, both domestic and international, which added layers of complexity to an already convoluted scenario.

Dilma Rousseff, a former guerrilla fighter who had been tortured under Brazil's military dictatorship, became the country's first female president in 2011. Her presidency was marked by efforts to continue the progressive policies of her predecessor, Luiz Inácio Lula da Silva, particularly in areas such as poverty reduction and economic growth. However, her tenure was also beset by economic difficulties, declining approval ratings, and burgeoning corruption scandals, most notably the Lava Jato (Operation Car Wash) investigation that uncovered widespread corruption involving the state oil company Petrobras and numerous political figures.

The immediate cause for Rousseff's impeachment was her alleged manipulation of government accounts to hide the extent of the country's fiscal deficits during her re-election campaign in 2014. This practice, known as "pedaladas fiscais" (fiscal pedaling), involved delaying payments to state banks to make the government's financial situation appear better than it actually was. Critics argued that this was a violation of fiscal responsibility laws, while Rousseff and her supporters contended that such maneuvers were common among previous administrations and did not constitute an impeachable offense.

Amid this political turmoil, suspicions of espionage emerged, further complicating the narrative. Reports surfaced suggesting that elements within the Brazilian intelligence community, as well as foreign intelligence agencies, had been involved in monitoring and possibly influencing political events in the country. These suspicions were fueled by several factors, including Brazil's significant geopolitical position, its natural resources, and its role as a leading economy in Latin America.

One of the key incidents highlighting concerns about espionage involved revelations by former NSA contractor Edward Snowden in 2013. The leaked documents indicated that the U.S. National Security Agency (NSA) had conducted extensive surveillance on Brazilian officials, including Rousseff herself. The surveillance reportedly targeted Rousseff's communications, as well as those of other high-ranking officials and Petrobras. This disclosure caused a diplomatic rift between Brazil and the United States, with Rousseff postponing a state visit to Washington in protest and publicly condemning the espionage as a violation of Brazilian sovereignty.

Domestically, the Brazilian Intelligence Agency (ABIN) was also suspected of engaging in surveillance activities. Reports indicated that ABIN might have been monitoring political opponents, activists, and even members of Rousseff's administration. The extent and nature of this domestic espionage remain unclear, but the atmosphere of mistrust and paranoia it generated contributed to the already tense political climate.

The impeachment proceedings against Rousseff began in late 2015, gaining momentum in 2016. The process was marked by intense political maneuvering, public protests, and deep divisions within Brazilian society. Supporters of the impeachment, primarily from opposition parties, argued that Rousseff's actions constituted a clear breach of fiscal responsibility and justified her removal from office. Opponents, however, claimed that the impeachment was a politically motivated coup, aimed at ousting a democratically elected leader and undermining the progressive agenda she represented.

As the impeachment process unfolded, allegations of espionage and political intrigue continued to surface. There were claims that segments of the Brazilian political elite, including figures from within Rousseff's own Workers' Party (PT), had conspired with opposition leaders and business interests to engineer her downfall. These claims were difficult to substantiate fully, but they added to the sense of a shadowy struggle for power playing out behind the scenes.

On August 31, 2016, the Brazilian Senate voted to impeach Dilma Rousseff, removing her from office. She was found guilty of fiscal mismanagement by a vote of 61 to 20, though she was allowed to retain her political rights, which meant she could still hold public office in the future. Her removal marked the end of 13 years of Workers' Party rule in Brazil and the beginning of a new political era under her vice president, Michel Temer, who had turned against her and allied with the opposition.

Rousseff's impeachment had profound and lasting effects on Brazil's political landscape. It deepened political polarization and distrust among the populace, eroded faith in democratic institutions, and triggered widespread protests and civil unrest. The episode also had significant economic repercussions, contributing to Brazil's ongoing struggles with recession and economic instability.

The broader context of espionage allegations and intelligence activities remains a murky and contentious aspect of Rousseff's impeachment. The disclosures of NSA surveillance underscored the extent to which global powers were involved in monitoring political developments in Brazil. Domestically, the potential role of ABIN and other intelligence actors in the political drama added to the complexity and opacity of the situation.

In the years following her impeachment, Dilma Rousseff has continued to be a vocal critic of the process that led to her ouster, describing it as a coup and a miscarriage of justice. She has also been an advocate for greater transparency and accountability in both domestic and international intelligence operations, emphasizing the need for protecting democratic processes from covert interference.

The impeachment of Dilma Rousseff serves as a powerful reminder of the intricate interplay between politics, intelligence, and international relations. It highlights how internal political struggles can be influenced by external forces and how allegations of espionage can exacerbate existing tensions and conflicts. The episode remains a contentious chapter in Brazil's history, reflecting the challenges of maintaining democratic governance in the face of economic crises, political corruption, and the ever-present shadow of intelligence operations.

Chapter 36: The Arrest of Robert Hanssen

The arrest of Robert Hanssen in 2001 was one of the most significant espionage cases in the history of the FBI, revealing the depth of the breach within America's premier law enforcement and intelligence agency. Hanssen, an FBI agent, had been spying for the Soviet Union and later Russia for over two decades, compromising some of the United States' most sensitive secrets and intelligence operations. His betrayal exposed severe flaws in the FBI's internal security and counterintelligence procedures and had far-reaching implications for U.S. national security.

Robert Philip Hanssen was born on April 18, 1944, in Chicago, Illinois. He joined the FBI in 1976 after a stint with the Chicago Police Department. Initially, Hanssen's work at the FBI was unremarkable, but his career trajectory changed dramatically when he was assigned to counterintelligence in New York City in 1979. This position provided him access to highly classified information about U.S. intelligence operations against the Soviet Union. It was around this time that Hanssen began his espionage activities.

In 1979, Hanssen approached the Soviet military intelligence agency, the GRU, offering to sell classified information. He initially used the alias "Ramon Garcia" and communicated with his handlers through dead drops and encrypted communications, employing elaborate tradecraft to avoid detection. Hanssen's motivations appeared to be a combination of financial greed and a desire for recognition. Over the years, he received over $1.4 million in cash and diamonds for his services, although he lived modestly to avoid suspicion.

Hanssen's espionage activities were extensive and devastating. He compromised numerous intelligence operations, including a highly sensitive operation involving the monitoring of Soviet communication systems. One of the most significant betrayals was his disclosure of the identities of three Russian agents working for the United States: General Dmitri Polyakov, Sergei Motorin, and Valery Martynov. All three were executed by the Soviet Union as a result of Hanssen's betrayal. He also provided the Soviets with detailed information about U.S. nuclear war plans, counterintelligence operations, and the identities of dozens of covert operatives.

Despite the severe consequences of his actions, Hanssen managed to avoid detection for many years. His success was partly due to his meticulous methods and the FBI's lack of robust internal security measures. He used a variety of techniques to evade suspicion, including using anonymous letters, coded messages, and sophisticated encryption. He also took advantage of the bureaucratic nature of the FBI, ensuring that no single individual had a complete picture of his activities.

Hanssen's ability to remain undetected was also due to the compartmentalization of information within the FBI. Different divisions did not share intelligence freely, creating gaps in oversight that Hanssen exploited. Furthermore, the culture within the FBI at the time was such that internal security was not given the priority it needed. There was a presumption that FBI agents were inherently trustworthy, which allowed Hanssen to operate with minimal scrutiny.

The break in the case came in the late 1990s when the FBI and the CIA launched a joint investigation to find a mole responsible for significant intelligence losses. The investigation, codenamed "Gray Suit," involved an exhaustive review of intelligence leaks, counterintelligence failures, and the few leads they had. They focused on identifying anomalies in the conduct of employees with access to sensitive information. During this period, suspicions began to narrow down to Hanssen, although concrete evidence was still lacking.

A significant breakthrough came in 2000 when the FBI received a valuable tip from a former KGB operative who had defected to the

United States. This informant provided the FBI with a substantial amount of information, including a file containing details about the mole. The file included a tape recording of a conversation between the mole and his Soviet handlers, as well as copies of letters the mole had written. The voice on the tape was identified as Hanssen's, and the handwriting on the letters matched his.

With this crucial evidence, the FBI launched a covert surveillance operation to monitor Hanssen's activities. They installed surveillance cameras and listening devices in his office and home and tracked his movements closely. They discovered that Hanssen was still actively engaged in espionage, and they decided to catch him in the act to ensure a watertight case.

On February 18, 2001, Hanssen was arrested at Foxstone Park near his home in Vienna, Virginia. He was caught red-handed making a dead drop of classified materials for his Russian handlers. The FBI had planted false information to bait Hanssen, ensuring that the materials he was dropping did not compromise any current operations. His arrest marked the culmination of an intense and secretive investigation and brought an end to one of the most damaging espionage careers in U.S. history.

Following his arrest, Hanssen was charged with multiple counts of espionage and conspiracy. He initially pleaded not guilty but later entered a plea agreement to avoid the death penalty. In exchange for his cooperation and full disclosure of his espionage activities, he received a sentence of life in prison without the possibility of parole. Hanssen was incarcerated at the ADX Florence, a federal supermax prison in Colorado, where he remains to this day.

The Hanssen case had profound implications for the FBI and the broader U.S. intelligence community. It exposed significant weaknesses in internal security and counterintelligence practices, leading to a comprehensive overhaul of these systems. The FBI established new protocols for monitoring employees with access to sensitive information, including more rigorous background checks, periodic polygraph tests, and enhanced surveillance of high-risk individuals.

The case also underscored the importance of interagency cooperation in counterintelligence efforts. The joint FBI-CIA task force that ultimately exposed Hanssen demonstrated the effectiveness of collaborative approaches to complex intelligence challenges. It highlighted the need for better information sharing and coordination among various intelligence and law enforcement agencies to identify and neutralize internal threats.

Furthermore, the Hanssen case served as a cautionary tale about the potential for betrayal within even the most trusted institutions. It illustrated how personal motivations, such as financial gain and a desire for recognition, could drive individuals to commit acts of treason. The case also emphasized the need for continuous vigilance and robust security measures to protect national security interests.

In the aftermath of Hanssen's arrest, the FBI made significant efforts to rebuild trust and credibility both within the agency and with the public. They conducted internal reviews to identify and address systemic weaknesses, implemented new training programs for counterintelligence officers, and fostered a culture of accountability and transparency. These measures aimed to prevent similar breaches in the future and to restore confidence in the FBI's ability to safeguard national security.

The arrest of Robert Hanssen remains a pivotal moment in the history of U.S. intelligence and counterintelligence operations. It revealed the vulnerabilities of even the most secure institutions and underscored the necessity of constant vigilance and robust security measures. Hanssen's actions had far-reaching consequences, compromising critical intelligence operations and endangering the lives of numerous operatives. His case serves as a stark reminder of the ever-present threat of espionage and the ongoing efforts required to protect national security in an increasingly complex and interconnected world.

Chapter 37: Operation Northwoods: False Flag Proposals

Operation Northwoods is one of the most striking examples of proposed false flag operations in American history. Devised in 1962 by the United States Department of Defense and the Joint Chiefs of Staff, this covert plan sought to orchestrate acts of terrorism on American soil and blame them on the Cuban government. The objective was to create a pretext for the United States to invade Cuba and overthrow its leader, Fidel Castro. While the operation was never executed, its very conception reveals the lengths to which some elements of the U.S. government were willing to go during the Cold War to counteract the perceived threat of communism in the Western Hemisphere.

The backdrop to Operation Northwoods was the Cuban Revolution and the rise of Fidel Castro, who overthrew the U.S.-backed dictator Fulgencio Batista in 1959. Castro's establishment of a communist government aligned with the Soviet Union alarmed the United States, particularly given Cuba's proximity to American shores. The subsequent nationalization of American-owned businesses and properties in Cuba, along with Castro's anti-American rhetoric, further strained relations.

In response, the U.S. government initiated various efforts to undermine and destabilize Castro's regime. One of the most notable early attempts was the Bay of Pigs invasion in April 1961, a failed military invasion of Cuba undertaken by Cuban exiles with the backing of the CIA. The disastrous outcome of the invasion not only embarrassed the United States but also strengthened Castro's position and pushed Cuba closer to the Soviet Union. In the aftermath, the Kennedy administration sought alternative means to remove Castro from power, leading to the development of more aggressive and clandestine strategies.

Operation Northwoods emerged from this context. Drafted in March 1962 by the Joint Chiefs of Staff under the leadership of Chairman General Lyman Lemnitzer, the plan proposed a series of staged incidents intended to deceive the American public and the international community into supporting military action against Cuba. These incidents were to be crafted to appear as Cuban aggression, thereby justifying U.S. intervention. The proposed operations included a wide range of deceptive tactics, each more shocking than the last.

One of the key elements of Operation Northwoods was the idea of staging attacks on American military and civilian targets and then attributing these attacks to Cuban operatives. These attacks included scenarios such as hijacking American aircraft, sinking ships, and conducting bombings in U.S. cities. The goal was to create a sense of crisis and outrage that would galvanize public and political support for a military invasion of Cuba.

Specific proposals within Operation Northwoods were chillingly detailed. For instance, one plan involved the simulation of a Cuban attack on Guantanamo Bay, the U.S. naval base in Cuba. This could include blowing up ammunition stores, setting fires, and even arranging for the deaths of American servicemen to make the attack appear authentic. Another plan suggested the possibility of sinking a boatload of Cuban refugees en route to Florida, creating a humanitarian tragedy that could be blamed on Castro.

Additionally, the plan proposed faking a shoot-down of a civilian airliner, an idea that involved creating a scenario where a chartered aircraft, filled with college students or other civilians, would be purportedly shot down by Cuban forces. The document suggested that the actual aircraft could be substituted with a drone, while the real passengers would be secretly landed elsewhere. This gruesome idea was intended to shock the American public and build support for military action.

Operation Northwoods also included proposals to stage attacks using false uniforms and equipment, such as Cuban military planes painted to resemble American aircraft. This deception aimed to create confusion and conflict, making it appear that Cuban forces were engaging in acts of war against the United States. The plan even went as far as to consider the assassination of Cuban exiles in the United States to generate anti-Cuban sentiment.

The overall strategy of Operation Northwoods was rooted in the concept of false flag operations, a term used to describe covert activities designed to appear as if they were carried out by other entities. This tactic has been used throughout history to manipulate public opinion and justify military actions. The audacity and moral bankruptcy of such proposals reflect the intense pressure and desperation felt by U.S. policymakers at the height of the Cold War.

Despite the meticulous planning and detailed proposals, Operation Northwoods was ultimately rejected. When the plan was presented to Secretary of Defense Robert McNamara and President John F. Kennedy, it was met with disapproval. Kennedy, in particular, was reportedly horrified by the extent of the proposed deception and the potential for loss of innocent American lives. The president's refusal to authorize the operation marked a critical moment in the decision-making process and highlighted the ethical boundaries that even during intense geopolitical confrontations, some U.S. leaders were unwilling to cross.

The rejection of Operation Northwoods did not, however, put an end to U.S. efforts to undermine Castro's regime. Throughout the 1960s, the CIA continued to pursue a variety of covert operations under the umbrella of Operation Mongoose, which included sabotage, propaganda, and attempts to incite rebellion within Cuba. These efforts were part of a broader strategy to destabilize communist governments worldwide during the Cold War.

The existence of Operation Northwoods remained a closely guarded secret for many years. It was not until the 1990s that the details of the plan were declassified and became publicly known. The revelation of such a plan shocked many and sparked debates about the ethical limits of government actions in the name of national security. It also added to the complex legacy of U.S. foreign policy during the Cold War, a period marked by both the defense of democratic ideals and the employment of morally dubious tactics.

Operation Northwoods stands as a stark reminder of the potential for abuse of power within government agencies, especially during times of heightened fear and tension. The plan's existence underscores the importance of transparency, accountability, and ethical considerations in the formulation of national security policies. It also serves as a cautionary tale about the dangers of allowing the ends to justify the means in matters of international relations and domestic security.

In the broader context of history, Operation Northwoods is a testament to the lengths to which governments may go to achieve strategic objectives, often at the expense of moral and ethical considerations. It highlights the perpetual tension between security and liberty, and the need for vigilance to ensure that the actions taken in the name of national defense do not undermine the very principles they are meant to protect. The rejection of Operation Northwoods by Kennedy also exemplifies the critical role of leadership and ethical judgment in guiding national policy, demonstrating that even in the face of existential threats, there are lines that should not be crossed.

Chapter 38: The Thawra in Yemen: Nasser's Proxy War

The Thawra in Yemen, also known as the North Yemen Civil War (1962-1970), was a significant conflict that played out as a proxy war largely driven by the ambitions and strategies of Gamal Abdel Nasser, the President of Egypt. Nasser sought to extend his influence throughout the Arab world, spreading the ideology of Arab nationalism and socialism. The conflict in Yemen became a focal point of Cold War geopolitics, pitting Nasser's Egypt against the Saudi Arabian monarchy and other conservative Arab regimes, with indirect involvement from the superpowers, the United States and the Soviet Union.

The origins of the Yemeni conflict can be traced back to the political dynamics within the country itself. North Yemen, officially the Mutawakkilite Kingdom of Yemen, was ruled by the Hamidaddin family under a traditional monarchy led by Imam Yahya and later his son, Imam Ahmad. The regime was conservative and maintained a strong alliance with tribal leaders and religious authorities. However, the kingdom was relatively isolated, economically underdeveloped, and politically stagnant, which sowed seeds of discontent among various segments of Yemeni society.

The death of Imam Ahmad in September 1962 marked a turning point. His son, Crown Prince Muhammad al-Badr, succeeded him, but his reign was immediately challenged. On September 26, 1962, a group of military officers inspired by Nasser's pan-Arabist and republican ideals staged a coup d'état, deposing al-Badr and proclaiming the establishment of the Yemen Arab Republic (YAR). The revolutionaries were led by Abdullah al-Sallal, who became the first President of the YAR. This coup triggered the Thawra, a civil war between the republican forces and royalist forces loyal to the deposed Imam.

Nasser quickly saw an opportunity to expand his influence in the Arabian Peninsula by supporting the Yemeni republicans. He dispatched military advisors, weapons, and eventually tens of thousands of Egyptian troops to support al-Sallal's government. Nasser's intervention was driven by his vision of uniting the Arab world under a single political and ideological banner. Yemen, strategically located on the Arabian Peninsula and adjacent to key maritime routes, was an important theater for this ambition.

On the opposing side, the royalists received significant support from Saudi Arabia, which viewed the spread of Nasser's revolutionary ideology as a direct threat to its own monarchy and the stability of the conservative Arab states. The Saudis provided the royalists with financial aid, weapons, and logistical support. This external backing turned the civil war into a protracted and bloody conflict, with both sides receiving substantial foreign assistance.

The war was characterized by brutal and often unconventional warfare. The terrain of North Yemen, with its rugged mountains and difficult landscape, favored guerrilla tactics. The royalists, drawing on the support of tribal fighters familiar with the terrain, employed hit-and-run tactics, ambushes, and sabotage to great effect against the better-equipped but less mobile Egyptian forces. The conflict saw extensive use of air power by the Egyptians, including controversial use of chemical weapons in attempts to subdue the royalist strongholds.

Despite their initial successes and overwhelming numbers, the Egyptian forces found themselves bogged down in a quagmire. The Yemeni campaign turned into a costly and protracted conflict that drained Egyptian resources and morale. Nasser's intervention in Yemen became increasingly unpopular at home, particularly as the economic and human costs mounted. Estimates suggest that Egypt may have lost as many as 10,000 soldiers in Yemen, with many more wounded or incapacitated.

The conflict also had significant implications for regional and global geopolitics. The United States, wary of Nasser's growing influence and the spread of Soviet-backed socialism in the region, covertly supported the royalists through its allies, Saudi Arabia and Jordan. Meanwhile, the Soviet Union, despite its ideological alignment with Nasser, was cautious about becoming too deeply involved, offering limited support to Egypt but not engaging directly in the conflict.

The civil war dragged on through the 1960s, with neither side able to secure a decisive victory. The stalemate was exacerbated by the broader geopolitical context of the Cold War, where regional conflicts were often sustained by the competing interests of the superpowers. The war also saw the emergence of complex local dynamics, as various Yemeni factions and tribes aligned themselves with either the republicans or royalists based on shifting alliances, historical grievances, and pragmatic considerations.

A critical turning point came in 1967, with the Six-Day War between Israel and the coalition of Arab states led by Egypt, Jordan, and Syria. Egypt's defeat in this conflict significantly weakened Nasser's position and his ability to sustain the military effort in Yemen. The financial and military strain of the Yemeni intervention, combined with the humiliation of the defeat by Israel, forced Nasser to reassess his strategy.

In 1967, Nasser began to withdraw Egyptian troops from Yemen, a process that was completed by 1970. This withdrawal was part of a broader disengagement and a recognition of the limits of Egypt's capacity to project power in the region. The departure of Egyptian forces led to a gradual de-escalation of the conflict, although sporadic fighting continued.

The end of direct Egyptian involvement allowed for a negotiated settlement to be reached. In 1970, a peace agreement was brokered that recognized the Yemen Arab Republic, but allowed for a degree of autonomy for royalist factions. This compromise brought an end to the civil war, although it did not resolve the underlying tensions and divisions within Yemeni society.

The Thawra in Yemen and Nasser's proxy war had lasting consequences for the region. The conflict exposed the vulnerabilities and limitations of Nasser's pan-Arabist vision and marked a significant blow to his ambitions. It also highlighted the complexities of Middle Eastern geopolitics, where local conflicts could be heavily influenced by external powers with competing interests. The war left Yemen deeply divided and underdeveloped, setting the stage for future conflicts and instability.

For Yemen, the civil war and its aftermath entrenched a pattern of external intervention and internal fragmentation that has continued to plague the country. The republican experiment that emerged from the conflict faced numerous challenges, including ongoing tribal unrest, economic difficulties, and regional rivalries. The legacy of the Thawra can be seen in the persistent struggles for power and the continuing influence of external actors in Yemen's affairs.

Nasser's involvement in Yemen, often referred to as "Egypt's Vietnam," serves as a cautionary tale about the perils of foreign intervention and the difficulties of imposing ideological visions on complex and diverse societies. It underscores the importance of understanding local dynamics and the risks of underestimating the resilience and motivations of indigenous forces.

The Thawra in Yemen remains a pivotal chapter in the history of the Arab world, reflecting the interplay of ideology, power, and geopolitics that has shaped the region's modern history. It is a reminder of the enduring impact of colonial legacies, the aspirations for independence and unity, and the often harsh realities of political and military conflicts in a volatile region.

Chapter 39: The Assassination of Reinhard Heydrich

The assassination of Reinhard Heydrich, one of the highest-ranking Nazi officials, is a historical event that exemplifies the bravery, complexity, and dire consequences of resistance movements during World War II. Codenamed Operation Anthropoid, this daring mission was orchestrated by the British Special Operations Executive (SOE) and executed by Czech and Slovak soldiers-in-exile with the goal of eliminating a key architect of the Holocaust and the Nazi regime's oppressive policies in occupied Czechoslovakia.

Reinhard Heydrich, often referred to as "The Butcher of Prague," held the position of Reich Protector of Bohemia and Moravia, the occupied territories of Czechoslovakia. He was a principal figure in the SS, the head of the Reich Main Security Office, and a key planner of the Final Solution, the Nazi plan to exterminate the Jews of Europe. His ruthless efficiency in suppressing resistance and implementing genocidal policies made him a prime target for the Allied forces and the Czechoslovak government-in-exile, which was led by President Edvard Beneš.

The decision to assassinate Heydrich was made in late 1941, amid growing frustration with the brutal Nazi occupation. The Czechoslovak government-in-exile, based in London, was eager to demonstrate its commitment to fighting the Nazis and to galvanize resistance within the occupied homeland. The SOE, established to conduct espionage, sabotage, and reconnaissance in occupied Europe, provided the training and logistical support for the operation.

The mission was entrusted to two Czechoslovak soldiers, Jozef Gabčík and Jan Kubiš, who were part of the Czechoslovak army-in-exile in Britain. They were rigorously trained in covert operations, including parachuting, combat, sabotage, and survival skills. In December 1941, they were parachuted into Czechoslovakia, along with other operatives, to begin preparations for the assassination.

The plan to kill Heydrich, known as Operation Anthropoid, involved detailed reconnaissance and coordination with local resistance networks. Gabčík and Kubiš had to navigate the challenges of operating in a heavily policed and hostile environment. They initially received assistance from the local resistance, which provided them with shelter, intelligence, and logistical support. Despite the risks, they persevered, recognizing the significance of their mission.

Heydrich was known for his predictable routine, which included regular commutes in an open-top car from his home to his office at Prague Castle. This pattern provided an opportunity for the operatives to plan an ambush. After weeks of surveillance and planning, the chosen location for the attack was a sharp bend in the road near the Bulovka Hospital in Prague's Kobylisy district. This spot forced vehicles to slow down, giving the assassins a brief window to strike.

On May 27, 1942, Gabčík and Kubiš lay in wait at the designated location. As Heydrich's car approached, Gabčík stepped into the road and aimed a Sten submachine gun at the vehicle. However, the gun jammed, and Gabčík was unable to fire. In a moment of quick thinking, Kubiš threw an anti-tank grenade, which exploded near the rear of the car. The explosion severely wounded Heydrich and caused significant damage to the vehicle.

Heydrich, though gravely injured, managed to exit the car and attempted to pursue the assassins on foot before collapsing. Gabčík and Kubiš, believing the mission had succeeded, fled the scene on bicycles and sought refuge with local resistance contacts. Heydrich was taken to the Bulovka Hospital, where he initially appeared to be recovering after emergency surgery. However, he succumbed to his injuries on June 4, 1942, due to sepsis caused by shrapnel and debris in his wounds.

The assassination of Heydrich, though a tactical success, triggered a brutal and immediate Nazi retaliation. The regime, determined to crush any semblance of resistance, launched a campaign of terror across Czechoslovakia. Heinrich Himmler, Heydrich's superior and head of the SS, ordered a massive crackdown. Thousands of suspected resistance members and sympathizers were arrested, tortured, and executed. Entire villages, such as Lidice and Ležáky, were razed to the ground, and their inhabitants were either killed or deported to concentration camps.

The hunt for the assassins and their supporters intensified. Despite the immense pressure, Gabčík and Kubiš, along with several other operatives, found temporary refuge in the crypt of the Church of Saints Cyril and Methodius in Prague. The Gestapo, using information extracted under torture from captured resistance members, eventually located their hideout. On June 18, 1942, a fierce gun battle ensued between the cornered operatives and a much larger German force.

After hours of resistance, the situation became untenable. Rather than surrendering, Gabčík, Kubiš, and their comrades chose to fight to the death. Kubiš was mortally wounded during the battle, and Gabčík and the others took their own lives to avoid capture. Their sacrifice became a symbol of defiance and bravery in the face of overwhelming oppression.

Operation Anthropoid had profound implications for the course of World War II and the perception of the Nazi occupation in Czechoslovakia. The assassination of Heydrich significantly disrupted the Nazi administration and delayed the implementation of some of the most draconian policies in the occupied territories. It also sent a powerful message to the world that the Czechoslovak people and their allies would not passively accept Nazi tyranny.

The operation's success in eliminating one of the most feared Nazi officials bolstered the morale of resistance movements across Europe. It demonstrated that even the most powerful figures in the Nazi regime were vulnerable to targeted actions. This encouraged other resistance groups to intensify their efforts against the occupiers, contributing to the broader Allied war effort.

However, the immediate aftermath of the operation was marked by extreme suffering and loss for the Czech population. The Nazi reprisals were devastating, and the destruction of Lidice and Ležáky became enduring symbols of Nazi brutality. The scale and ferocity of the reprisals shocked the world and further galvanized international opposition to the Nazi regime.

In the long term, Operation Anthropoid solidified the legacy of the Czechoslovak resistance and its contributions to the fight against Nazism. The courage and sacrifice of Gabčík, Kubiš, and their fellow operatives are commemorated in numerous memorials, museums, and cultural works. Their story serves as a poignant reminder of the high cost of resistance and the enduring human spirit in the face of tyranny.

The assassination of Reinhard Heydrich through Operation Anthropoid remains a defining episode in the history of World War II. It highlights the complex interplay of courage, strategy, and sacrifice that characterized the resistance movements against Nazi occupation. The operation's impact reverberated far beyond Czechoslovakia, influencing the broader dynamics of the war and shaping the historical memory of resistance and resilience in the face of overwhelming odds.

Chapter 40: The 9/11 Attacks

The 9/11 attacks, a series of coordinated terrorist acts carried out by the extremist group al-Qaeda on September 11, 2001, stand as one of the most pivotal events in modern history, significantly shaping global geopolitics and international security policies. The attacks targeted symbols of American power and aimed to instill fear and chaos across the United States and the world. On that fateful morning, nineteen terrorists hijacked four commercial airplanes. Two of these planes, American Airlines Flight 11 and United Airlines Flight 175, were deliberately crashed into the North and South Towers of the World Trade Center in New York City, causing the iconic skyscrapers to collapse within hours. Another plane, American Airlines Flight 77, was flown into the Pentagon, the heart of the U.S. Department of Defense, in Arlington, Virginia. The fourth plane, United Airlines Flight 93, was intended to strike another major target in Washington, D.C., possibly the White House or the Capitol. However, passengers on Flight 93 fought back against the hijackers, leading the plane to crash into a field in Pennsylvania instead.

The immediate aftermath of the attacks was catastrophic. Nearly 3,000 people were killed, including first responders who rushed to the scenes to save lives. The destruction of the World Trade Center resulted in a massive debris field and a persistent plume of toxic dust that affected the health of rescue workers and residents in the vicinity for years. The psychological impact on the American populace and the world was profound, with images of the collapsing towers and the Pentagon engulfed in flames being etched into collective memory.

In response to the 9/11 attacks, the United States swiftly launched the War on Terror, a global military campaign aimed at dismantling terrorist networks and preventing future attacks. This led to the invasion of Afghanistan in October 2001, where the ruling Taliban regime was harboring Osama bin Laden, the mastermind behind the attacks, and his al-Qaeda network. The U.S.-led coalition quickly ousted the Taliban from power, but the conflict morphed into a prolonged insurgency, with international forces and Afghan security personnel battling Taliban fighters for nearly two decades.

The intelligence and security apparatus of the United States underwent significant restructuring in the wake of 9/11. The Department of Homeland Security was established, consolidating various federal agencies to better coordinate efforts to protect the nation. The USA PATRIOT Act was enacted, expanding the surveillance and investigative powers of law enforcement agencies to thwart potential terrorist activities. These measures sparked intense debates over civil liberties and the balance between security and privacy.

Osama bin Laden, the figurehead of al-Qaeda, evaded capture for nearly a decade. The search for him involved an extensive network of intelligence operatives, advanced surveillance technologies, and collaboration with foreign governments. In 2011, the United States finally located bin Laden in a fortified compound in Abbottabad, Pakistan. On May 2, 2011, U.S. Navy SEALs conducted a daring nighttime raid, codenamed Operation Neptune Spear, resulting in the death of bin Laden. His body was swiftly buried at sea to prevent his grave from becoming a shrine for extremists. This operation was a significant morale boost for the United States and its allies, symbolizing a major victory in the War on Terror.

The 9/11 attacks also prompted widespread changes in global aviation security. Measures such as reinforced cockpit doors, enhanced passenger screening procedures, and the establishment of the Transportation Security Administration (TSA) were implemented to prevent hijackings and ensure the safety of air travel. International cooperation in counterterrorism efforts increased, with countries sharing intelligence and coordinating actions to disrupt terrorist cells and financing networks.

Beyond the immediate security responses, the 9/11 attacks had far-reaching geopolitical consequences. The invasion of Iraq in 2003, justified by the Bush administration as part of the broader War on Terror, led to the toppling of Saddam Hussein but also sparked a violent insurgency and sectarian conflict, destabilizing the region. The spread of extremist ideologies and the rise of groups like ISIS can be traced back, in part, to the power vacuums and social upheavals that followed the U.S. interventions in the Middle East.

Domestically, the attacks influenced American society and politics in numerous ways. They fostered a sense of national unity and resilience but also contributed to a climate of fear and suspicion, particularly towards Muslim and Arab communities. The subsequent increase in hate crimes and discriminatory policies highlighted the complex interplay between security concerns and civil rights.

In popular culture, the events of 9/11 and their aftermath have been depicted in countless books, films, and documentaries, reflecting ongoing attempts to process and understand the tragedy. Memorials such as the National September 11 Memorial & Museum in New York City serve as poignant reminders of the lives lost and the enduring impact of that day.

The 9/11 attacks were a watershed moment in contemporary history, reshaping international relations, security policies, and societal attitudes. The death of Osama bin Laden, while a significant milestone, did not mark the end of the challenges posed by terrorism. The legacy of 9/11 continues to influence the global landscape, reminding us of the ongoing need for vigilance, cooperation, and a nuanced approach to addressing the root causes of extremism.

Chapter 41: The Bletchley Park Codebreakers

Bletchley Park, the British codebreaking center during World War II, played a pivotal role in the Allied victory by deciphering encrypted German communications. Among the many individuals who contributed to the success of Bletchley Park, women were integral, representing a significant portion of the workforce. Their contributions, often overshadowed by their male counterparts, were vital to the codebreaking efforts and espionage activities. The story of these women in espionage at Bletchley Park is one of dedication, skill, and unsung heroism.

Women at Bletchley Park were recruited from various backgrounds, including university graduates, schoolteachers, linguists, and even young debutantes who had come out to society. The recruitment process was unconventional; it often relied on word of mouth and personal recommendations rather than formal advertisements. Women who showed aptitude in languages, mathematics, or logic were identified and recruited into the codebreaking operations. The urgency of war necessitated the inclusion of women in roles that had traditionally been reserved for men, marking a significant shift in societal norms.

One of the most notable women at Bletchley Park was Joan Clarke. Clarke, a mathematician and cryptanalyst, worked alongside Alan Turing in Hut 8, which was responsible for breaking the German Naval Enigma. Despite the gender biases of the time, Clarke's exceptional mathematical skills earned her a crucial role in deciphering the complex codes used by the German navy. She made significant contributions to the development of methods for breaking the Enigma, including the use of statistical techniques and the design of cryptographic systems.

Clarke's work was instrumental in the success of Operation Ultra, which provided critical intelligence to the Allied forces.

Another prominent figure was Mavis Batey, a gifted linguist who played a key role in deciphering the Italian Naval Enigma and the German Lorenz cipher. Batey's breakthrough in decoding a message related to the Italian fleet's movements led to the decisive Allied victory at the Battle of Cape Matapan in 1941. Her work on the Lorenz cipher, a more complex system than the Enigma, was crucial in understanding the high-level strategic communications of the German High Command. Batey's contributions were vital to the success of several major Allied operations and underscored the importance of linguistic skills in codebreaking.

Women at Bletchley Park were not limited to the role of cryptanalysts. Many served as clerks, typists, and machine operators, handling the vast amounts of intercepted enemy communications. These roles were essential for the smooth functioning of the codebreaking process. The Women's Royal Naval Service (WRNS), commonly known as Wrens, played a significant role in operating the Bombe machines, which were used to mechanize the process of breaking Enigma codes. The meticulous work of these women in setting up and maintaining the machines was crucial in the timely decryption of messages, providing the Allies with valuable intelligence.

The women at Bletchley Park also faced numerous challenges and hardships. The work was highly demanding, often involving long hours and intense pressure to deliver results. The secrecy surrounding their work meant they could not discuss it with anyone, including their families. This isolation was compounded by the fact that many women had to live away from home, often in austere conditions. Despite these challenges, the women of Bletchley Park remained dedicated to their work, driven by a sense of duty and the knowledge that their efforts were contributing to the war effort.

The contributions of women at Bletchley Park extended beyond codebreaking. Many were involved in the dissemination of intelligence, ensuring that decrypted messages were passed on to the relevant military and government authorities. This work required a high degree of discretion and accuracy, as even the smallest error could have significant consequences. Women also played a role in analyzing the decrypted messages, providing context and insights that were critical for strategic planning.

The impact of the women at Bletchley Park was profound. Their work shortened the war and saved countless lives by providing the Allies with the information needed to anticipate and counter German operations. The intelligence gathered at Bletchley Park influenced major events such as the Battle of the Atlantic, the D-Day landings, and the North African campaign. The success of these operations hinged on the timely and accurate intelligence produced by the codebreakers, many of whom were women.

Despite their significant contributions, the women of Bletchley Park received little recognition during or immediately after the war. The official secrets act, which bound all personnel to secrecy, meant that their achievements remained largely unknown for decades. It was only in recent years that the full extent of their contributions has been acknowledged and celebrated. The stories of Joan Clarke, Mavis Batey, and countless other women have finally come to light, highlighting their crucial role in the success of Bletchley Park.

The legacy of the women at Bletchley Park extends beyond their wartime contributions. Their work challenged traditional gender roles and paved the way for greater inclusion of women in science, technology, engineering, and mathematics (STEM) fields. The skills and experience gained by these women during the war allowed many to pursue successful careers in academia, government, and industry. Their achievements continue to inspire future generations of women to pursue careers in fields that were once dominated by men.

Chapter 42: The Litvinenko Poisoning

The Litvinenko poisoning case is one of the most notorious examples of state-sponsored assassination on foreign soil. Alexander Litvinenko, a former officer of the Russian Federal Security Service (FSB), fled to the United Kingdom in 2000 after becoming a vocal critic of the Russian government. He sought asylum in the UK and continued his opposition to the Kremlin from abroad. His assassination in 2006, through the use of a rare radioactive substance, polonium-210, shocked the world and brought attention to the lengths to which the Russian state might go to silence its critics.

Alexander Litvinenko's career in the FSB saw him involved in investigating organized crime and corruption within the Russian government. However, his tenure became tumultuous when he publicly accused his superiors of ordering the assassination of Russian oligarch Boris Berezovsky. Litvinenko's allegations, combined with his criticisms of the FSB and President Vladimir Putin, made him a target for retribution. Fearing for his life, he fled to the United Kingdom, where he was granted asylum. In the UK, Litvinenko continued to work against the Russian state, collaborating with British intelligence and writing about the connections between the Russian government and organized crime.

On November 1, 2006, Litvinenko suddenly fell ill after a meeting at a London hotel with two former Russian security agents, Andrei Lugovoi and Dmitry Kovtun. Initially, his symptoms were perplexing, as they did not match any common illness. Litvinenko experienced severe gastrointestinal distress, hair loss, and a rapid decline in health. His condition baffled doctors until it was determined that he had been poisoned with polonium-210, a highly radioactive and extremely rare isotope. This revelation turned his illness into an international incident, as it indicated a sophisticated and state-sponsored assassination.

The use of polonium-210 as a poison was unprecedented. Polonium-210 is highly toxic, emitting alpha particles that cause massive damage to living cells when ingested or inhaled. Its presence in Litvinenko's body pointed to a deliberate and calculated act of murder, given the difficulty in acquiring and handling such a substance. The investigation into Litvinenko's death quickly identified Andrei Lugovoi and Dmitry Kovtun as the primary suspects. Traces of polonium-210 were found in various locations they had visited, including the hotel where they met Litvinenko and on the planes they traveled on. These findings supported the hypothesis that they had administered the poison during their meeting.

Litvinenko's deathbed statement explicitly accused President Vladimir Putin of orchestrating his assassination. This accusation was bolstered by the findings of a public inquiry in the UK, which concluded in 2016 that the killing was "probably approved" by Putin and FSB chief Nikolai Patrushev. The inquiry report detailed the events leading up to Litvinenko's death, the involvement of Lugovoi and Kovtun, and the evidence suggesting state sponsorship. The UK government, in response to the findings, condemned the assassination and called for the extradition of Lugovoi and Kovtun from Russia. However, the Russian government refused to comply, denying any involvement and dismissing the inquiry's conclusions.

The Litvinenko poisoning strained diplomatic relations between the UK and Russia. The UK expelled several Russian diplomats, and in turn, Russia expelled British diplomats. The incident highlighted the dangerous nature of Russian intelligence operations abroad and underscored the risks faced by dissidents and defectors. It also exposed the willingness of the Russian state to use lethal force beyond its borders to eliminate perceived threats.

The broader implications of the Litvinenko case are significant. It set a precedent for the use of exotic poisons in political assassinations and demonstrated the Kremlin's reach and ruthlessness. The case also underscored the vulnerability of defectors and critics of the Russian government, emphasizing the need for robust protection measures for individuals who flee authoritarian regimes. Furthermore, it raised concerns about the proliferation of radioactive materials and the potential for their use in targeted killings or terrorist attacks.

In addition to the political and diplomatic fallout, the Litvinenko case had personal ramifications for his family. Marina Litvinenko, Alexander's widow, became a vocal advocate for justice, tirelessly campaigning for an inquiry into her husband's death and seeking accountability from the Russian government. Her efforts brought significant public and media attention to the case, ensuring that it remained in the spotlight long after the initial incident.

The Litvinenko assassination also had a chilling effect on other Russian dissidents and former intelligence officers living in exile. It served as a stark warning that the reach of the Russian state extends far beyond its borders and that critics are never truly safe, even in countries that offer asylum and protection. This reality has led to heightened security measures for high-profile defectors and increased scrutiny of Russian activities abroad.

The use of polonium-210 in the assassination underscored the sophistication and resources available to Russian intelligence agencies. Polonium-210 is not only difficult to produce but also requires specialized knowledge to handle safely. The successful use of such a substance in an assassination plot demonstrated the capabilities of the Russian state and its willingness to deploy unconventional methods to achieve its objectives.

In the years following Litvinenko's death, other incidents have further illustrated the pattern of Russian state-sponsored assassinations. The poisoning of Sergei Skripal, a former Russian military intelligence officer, and his daughter Yulia in Salisbury, UK, in 2018 with a nerve agent known as Novichok, bore striking similarities to the Litvinenko case. The Skripal poisoning reinforced the perception that the Kremlin continues to target its adversaries with impunity, employing sophisticated and lethal methods.

The Litvinenko poisoning case remains a landmark event in the history of espionage and political assassination. It exposed the extent of Russian intelligence operations abroad and highlighted the persistent threat posed by state-sponsored assassinations. The case also demonstrated the challenges faced by democracies in protecting individuals from such threats and holding accountable those responsible. Despite the passage of time, the Litvinenko assassination continues to resonate, serving as a stark reminder of the dangerous interplay between politics, intelligence, and personal vendettas on the global stage.

Chapter 43: Operation Orchard

Operation Orchard, also known as Operation Outside the Box, was a clandestine Israeli military operation that took place on September 6, 2007. The operation involved an airstrike on a suspected nuclear reactor in the Deir ez-Zor region of Syria. This covert mission, carried out by the Israeli Air Force (IAF), aimed to eliminate what was believed to be a plutonium-producing reactor being constructed with North Korean assistance. The successful execution of Operation Orchard not only averted a potential nuclear threat but also underscored the complexities of modern intelligence, international diplomacy, and preemptive military action.

The genesis of Operation Orchard can be traced back to 2004 when Israeli intelligence began to suspect that Syria was pursuing a clandestine nuclear weapons program. These suspicions were fueled by satellite images and various intelligence reports indicating the construction of a facility in the remote region of Deir ez-Zor. The facility's design and layout bore a striking resemblance to North Korea's Yongbyon nuclear reactor, which further heightened Israeli concerns about potential North Korean involvement.

The breakthrough came in 2006 when Mossad, Israel's national intelligence agency, obtained photographs from a source within Syria that showed senior North Korean scientists and engineers present at the construction site. These images, coupled with other intelligence, convinced Israeli leaders that the facility was indeed a nuclear reactor intended for weapons production. The intelligence community, including Mossad and the Israeli Military Intelligence Directorate (Aman), conducted a thorough analysis and concluded that the reactor was nearing completion and posed a significant threat.

The decision to launch a preemptive strike was not taken lightly. Israeli Prime Minister Ehud Olmert, along with senior military and intelligence officials, debated the potential ramifications of the operation. There were significant risks involved, including the possibility of triggering a broader conflict with Syria and backlash from the international community. However, the potential threat of a nuclear-armed Syria outweighed these risks. The decision was made to proceed with a covert airstrike to ensure the reactor was destroyed before it became operational.

The planning and execution of Operation Orchard were meticulous. The Israeli Air Force assembled a squadron of F-15 and F-16 fighter jets, equipped with advanced electronic warfare systems to evade Syrian air defenses. On the night of September 6, 2007, the operation commenced. The Israeli jets flew low to avoid radar detection, traversing a route that minimized their exposure to Syrian air defenses. Electronic warfare systems were deployed to jam Syrian radar, ensuring that the jets remained undetected until they reached their target.

The strike itself was swift and precise. The Israeli jets dropped precision-guided bombs on the facility, completely destroying the reactor. The entire operation took less than an hour, and the Israeli jets returned to base without incident. The destruction of the reactor was confirmed by satellite imagery, which showed the facility reduced to rubble.

In the aftermath of the strike, both Israel and Syria adopted a policy of silence. Israel did not officially acknowledge its role in the operation until 2018, maintaining a policy of ambiguity to avoid escalating tensions. Syria, on the other hand, did not retaliate militarily but instead sought to downplay the incident, referring to the destroyed facility as an unused military building. The lack of immediate retaliation from Syria was partly due to the secretive nature of the reactor and the regime's desire to avoid drawing international scrutiny to its clandestine nuclear activities.

Internationally, the strike had significant implications. The United States, which had been kept informed about the operation, publicly supported Israel's right to defend itself against potential nuclear threats. The successful execution of Operation Orchard sent a clear message to other nations in the region about Israel's willingness and capability to carry out preemptive strikes to ensure its security. It also highlighted the proliferation concerns regarding North Korea's involvement in nuclear technology transfer to rogue states.

The operation sparked a debate about the efficacy and legality of preemptive strikes. Proponents argued that Operation Orchard was a necessary and justified action to prevent a hostile regime from acquiring nuclear weapons, thus ensuring regional and global security. Critics, however, contended that such unilateral military actions could undermine international norms and lead to increased instability. The debate also touched on the role of international institutions, such as the International Atomic Energy Agency (IAEA), in monitoring and preventing nuclear proliferation.

In the years following the strike, further details emerged about the extent of North Korean involvement in the Syrian reactor project. It became evident that North Korea had provided critical technical expertise and components for the reactor, underscoring the global nature of nuclear proliferation networks. This revelation prompted renewed calls for stricter international controls and sanctions to curb the spread of nuclear technology.

Operation Orchard also had significant ramifications for Israeli defense strategy and regional security dynamics. The operation demonstrated Israel's intelligence capabilities and its readiness to take decisive action against emerging threats. It reinforced the concept of preemptive strikes as a cornerstone of Israeli defense policy, particularly concerning non-conventional threats. The success of the operation likely deterred other adversaries in the region from pursuing similar clandestine nuclear programs, knowing that Israel would not hesitate to act.

The operation remains a case study in the complexities of modern warfare, intelligence, and international relations. It highlighted the importance of reliable intelligence in making critical national security decisions and the challenges associated with acting on that intelligence in a way that minimizes broader conflict. Operation Orchard exemplifies the delicate balance between preemptive action and diplomatic restraint, illustrating the difficult choices that nations must sometimes make to ensure their security.

Chapter 44: Operation Dark Heart: A Memoir Controversy

Operation Dark Heart: Spycraft and Special Ops on the Frontlines of Afghanistan and the Path to Victory is a memoir by Lieutenant Colonel Anthony Shaffer, published in 2010. The book chronicles Shaffer's experiences as an intelligence officer in Afghanistan, where he led a black-ops team known as Task Force Stratus Ivy. Shaffer's account offers an insider's perspective on the challenges and intricacies of intelligence operations during the early years of the Afghanistan war. However, the book became highly controversial due to its alleged disclosure of classified information, leading to significant legal and political battles, extensive redactions, and a broader debate about government transparency, censorship, and the public's right to know.

Anthony Shaffer, a veteran intelligence officer with over two decades of experience, wrote Operation Dark Heart to provide a detailed narrative of his deployment in Afghanistan in 2003. His memoir delves into the clandestine operations aimed at disrupting the Taliban and al-Qaeda networks. Shaffer's team worked on gathering actionable intelligence, conducting covert operations, and building alliances with Afghan tribal leaders. He offers vivid descriptions of the terrain, the cultural complexities, and the operational hazards faced by his unit. Through these accounts, Shaffer highlights both the successes and the frustrations of the intelligence community in navigating the turbulent landscape of Afghanistan.

Upon completing his manuscript, Shaffer submitted it for review to the Department of Defense (DoD), as required by military regulations for any publication by a current or former service member. Initially, the review process seemed routine, with Shaffer receiving approval from his immediate superiors. However, as the publication date approached, higher-level officials within the Pentagon and the intelligence community raised concerns about the content of the book. They claimed that the manuscript contained sensitive information that could compromise national security and endanger lives.

The controversy escalated when, after the book had already been printed and was ready for distribution, the DoD and the Central Intelligence Agency (CIA) intervened. They demanded significant redactions, citing that the memoir revealed classified details about intelligence sources, methods, and ongoing operations. This last-minute intervention led to the extraordinary step of purchasing and destroying the initial print run of 9,500 copies. The government's actions drew widespread media attention and ignited a public debate over censorship and the rights of authors, particularly those with military backgrounds.

The published version of Operation Dark Heart eventually contained over 200 redactions, making it a patchwork of blacked-out passages that left many sections of the narrative incomplete or incoherent. The redactions covered names, locations, operational details, and other elements deemed sensitive by the DoD and CIA. Shaffer and his supporters argued that much of the information censored in the book had already been available in the public domain through other sources. They contended that the excessive redactions were an attempt to suppress criticism of the military and intelligence agencies' handling of operations in Afghanistan.

One of the most contentious aspects of the memoir was Shaffer's account of the pre-9/11 intelligence efforts known as "Able Danger." According to Shaffer, Able Danger was a data-mining program that had identified key al-Qaeda operatives, including lead hijacker Mohamed Atta, before the September 11 attacks. Shaffer claimed that his attempts to share this information with the Federal Bureau of Investigation (FBI) were thwarted by bureaucratic obstacles and infighting between intelligence agencies. These assertions sparked a significant controversy, as they suggested that the attacks might have been preventable had the intelligence been acted upon more effectively.

The Able Danger revelations in Operation Dark Heart added fuel to the ongoing debate about intelligence failures leading up to 9/11. While some members of Congress and the public found Shaffer's claims compelling and called for further investigation, others within the intelligence community disputed his account, arguing that the program's findings were not as conclusive as Shaffer suggested. The controversy surrounding Able Danger became emblematic of the broader issues of information sharing and inter-agency cooperation within the U.S. intelligence apparatus.

The legal and political battles over Operation Dark Heart extended beyond the immediate controversy over the book's content. Shaffer faced personal and professional repercussions, including the revocation of his security clearance and his eventual retirement from the military under contentious circumstances. He continued to speak out about his experiences and the challenges faced by the intelligence community, becoming a vocal advocate for reform and greater transparency. The government's handling of Shaffer's case and the suppression of his memoir raised important questions about whistleblower protections and the balance between national security and freedom of speech.

The broader implications of the Operation Dark Heart controversy touched on the role of the media, publishers, and the public in scrutinizing government actions. The episode highlighted the tensions between the need for operational secrecy in intelligence work and the democratic imperative of accountability and transparency. It also underscored the challenges faced by authors with military or intelligence backgrounds in navigating the complex process of publishing their accounts, balancing the desire to share their experiences with the legal and ethical obligations to protect sensitive information.

In the years following the publication of Operation Dark Heart, the book and its controversy have continued to be a point of reference in discussions about government transparency, censorship, and the handling of classified information. The case has been cited in debates about the effectiveness and fairness of the pre-publication review process, the treatment of whistleblowers, and the public's right to know about the actions taken in their name. Shaffer's memoir, with its extensive redactions, stands as a symbol of the ongoing struggle to find the right balance between security and openness in a democratic society.

Chapter 45: The Arrest of Maria Butina

The arrest of Maria Butina, a Russian national, in July 2018 was a significant event in the realm of international espionage and political intrigue. Butina was charged with acting as an unregistered foreign agent for Russia, working to infiltrate influential political organizations in the United States, most notably the National Rifle Association (NRA), to advance Russian interests. Her case shed light on the sophisticated and subtle methods used by foreign intelligence services to influence American politics and policies from within, and it underscored the enduring complexities of U.S.-Russia relations in the post-Cold War era.

Maria Butina was born in Barnaul, Siberia, in 1988. She grew up in a typical Russian household and later moved to Moscow, where she established a career as a gun rights advocate. In 2011, she founded a pro-gun organization called Right to Bear Arms, which lobbied for the expansion of gun rights in Russia. This organization soon became a platform through which she could connect with influential figures both in Russia and internationally. Butina's work in this field brought her into contact with Alexander Torshin, a prominent Russian banker and a member of the Russian parliament with close ties to the Kremlin.

Alexander Torshin played a significant role in Butina's activities. As a senior official with deep connections in the Russian government, Torshin served as a mentor and sponsor to Butina, facilitating her entry into American political circles. The duo saw the NRA as a particularly strategic organization to infiltrate, given its considerable influence over American conservative politics and its extensive network of powerful allies, including politicians and businessmen. The NRA's connections to the Republican Party and its strong advocacy for gun rights made it an ideal target for influencing American policy and fostering pro-Russian sentiments among key decision-makers.

Butina first visited the United States in 2014, attending NRA conventions and establishing relationships with influential figures in the gun rights movement. She portrayed herself as a passionate advocate for gun rights, eager to learn from American activists to further her cause in Russia. This guise allowed her to build a network of contacts within the NRA and other conservative organizations. Butina's charm, intelligence, and dedication helped her gain access to high-profile events and meetings, where she mingled with prominent conservatives, including politicians, lobbyists, and influential NRA members.

Over the next few years, Butina continued to deepen her connections within the NRA and other conservative groups. She attended numerous NRA conventions, where she was often seen with top officials and prominent members. She also participated in various political events and conferences, including the National Prayer Breakfast, where she had opportunities to interact with influential political figures. Butina used these platforms to advocate for stronger U.S.-Russia relations, often framing her arguments in the context of shared values such as individual liberty and the right to bear arms.

In 2016, Butina enrolled as a graduate student at American University in Washington, D.C., further embedding herself in American society. She pursued a master's degree in international relations, which provided her with an academic cover and allowed her to continue her networking efforts. During her time at American University, Butina maintained regular contact with Torshin and other Russian officials, updating them on her activities and seeking guidance. These communications were later used as evidence of her clandestine efforts to influence U.S. policy on behalf of the Russian government.

Butina's activities drew the attention of U.S. law enforcement, and in July 2018, she was arrested and charged with conspiracy to act as an unregistered agent of a foreign government. The indictment detailed how Butina had worked under the direction of Torshin to infiltrate

American political organizations and influence U.S. policy towards Russia. The charges highlighted her efforts to develop relationships with influential political figures, attend high-profile events, and organize "friendship and dialogue" dinners to promote Russian interests.

The arrest of Maria Butina was a significant development in the context of ongoing investigations into Russian interference in the 2016 U.S. presidential election. Her case was separate from the broader investigation led by Special Counsel Robert Mueller, but it added to the growing body of evidence suggesting extensive Russian efforts to influence American politics. Butina's arrest came at a time of heightened scrutiny over foreign interference and raised questions about the vulnerability of American political organizations to infiltration by foreign agents.

During her trial, Butina initially pleaded not guilty, but in December 2018, she struck a plea deal with federal prosecutors. She admitted to conspiring to act as an unregistered foreign agent and agreed to cooperate with investigators. In her plea agreement, Butina acknowledged that she had worked with Torshin to cultivate relationships with American political figures and advance Russian interests. She admitted to using her connections within the NRA to gain access to influential conservatives and promote a pro-Russian agenda.

Butina's sentencing in April 2019 resulted in an 18-month prison term, which included time already served. The judge in her case noted the seriousness of her actions, stating that her efforts had the potential to cause significant harm to U.S. national security. After serving her sentence, Butina was deported to Russia in October 2019. Upon her return, she was welcomed as a hero by some in Russia, and she quickly reintegrated into public life, becoming a prominent commentator on Russian media and a member of the Russian parliament.

The Butina case had several far-reaching implications. Firstly, it highlighted the sophisticated methods used by foreign intelligence services to infiltrate and influence political organizations in other countries. Butina's ability to embed herself within the NRA and gain access to high-level political figures demonstrated the potential vulnerabilities of American institutions to foreign manipulation. Her case served as a wake-up call for political organizations and government agencies to strengthen their counterintelligence measures and ensure that foreign agents could not exploit their networks.

Secondly, the case underscored the ongoing efforts by the Russian government to influence American politics and policy. Butina's activities were part of a broader strategy by the Kremlin to cultivate relationships with influential Americans and shape U.S. policy in ways that favored Russian interests. The case added to the growing body of evidence suggesting that Russia was engaged in a concerted effort to undermine American democracy and sow discord within the United States.

Thirdly, the Butina case had significant political ramifications. It further strained U.S.-Russia relations, which were already tense due to allegations of Russian interference in the 2016 presidential election and other geopolitical issues. The case also fueled partisan divisions within the United States, with some viewing it as evidence of a broader conspiracy between the Trump campaign and Russia, while others saw it as an isolated incident. The political fallout from the case contributed to the ongoing debate over foreign interference in American politics and the need for robust measures to protect the integrity of U.S. democratic institutions.

Lastly, the Butina case raised important questions about the role of lobby groups and political organizations in American politics. The NRA, which had long been a powerful force in U.S. politics, faced scrutiny over its ties to Butina and potential vulnerabilities to foreign influence. The case prompted calls for greater transparency and oversight of lobbying activities and raised concerns about the influence of foreign money and interests in American political processes.

189

Chapter 46: The East German Stasi

The Ministry for State Security, commonly known as the Stasi, was the official state security service of the German Democratic Republic (GDR), or East Germany. Established in 1950 and dissolved in 1990 following the fall of the Berlin Wall, the Stasi is widely regarded as one of the most effective and repressive intelligence and secret police agencies in history. Its primary mission was to ensure the survival of the communist regime in East Germany through extensive surveillance, espionage, and suppression of dissent. The Stasi's methods and operations were vast and pervasive, affecting nearly every aspect of East German life, and its legacy continues to be a subject of significant historical inquiry and public interest.

The origins of the Stasi can be traced back to the immediate post-World War II period when East Germany was established as a Soviet satellite state. Modeled after the Soviet KGB, the Stasi was founded with the explicit purpose of safeguarding the socialist state against internal and external threats. Wilhelm Zaisser was appointed as the first head of the Stasi, but it was under his successor, Erich Mielke, that the organization truly expanded and became notorious. Mielke served as the Minister for State Security from 1957 until the collapse of the GDR in 1989, overseeing the growth and operations of the Stasi.

The Stasi's structure was hierarchical and complex, encompassing a wide range of departments and divisions dedicated to various aspects of state security. Its official headquarters, known as the Normannenstrasse complex, was located in East Berlin and served as the nerve center for its operations. At its peak, the Stasi employed over 90,000 full-time officers and approximately 170,000 informants, known as Inoffizielle Mitarbeiter (IMs), or unofficial collaborators. This vast network of informants included people from all walks of life, including neighbors, colleagues, friends, and even family members, who were coerced or persuaded to report on their fellow citizens.

One of the primary tools of the Stasi was its extensive surveillance apparatus. The agency meticulously monitored the East German population through a combination of physical surveillance, wiretaps, intercepted mail, and covert photography. Stasi officers conducted regular searches of homes and offices, often without the knowledge of the occupants. The agency maintained detailed files on millions of East Germans, cataloging their activities, associations, and suspected loyalties. By some estimates, the Stasi collected information on nearly a third of the East German population. These files were meticulously organized and stored, allowing the Stasi to quickly access and cross-reference information.

The Stasi also employed psychological techniques, known as Zersetzung, to intimidate, discredit, and destabilize perceived enemies of the state. Zersetzung involved a range of tactics designed to break the spirit of individuals, including spreading false rumors, manipulating personal relationships, and sabotaging careers. The goal was to isolate and demoralize targets, making them feel paranoid, helpless, and ostracized. This form of psychological warfare was often subtle and insidious, leaving no clear evidence of direct state intervention but causing significant distress and damage to the individuals involved.

In addition to its domestic operations, the Stasi was highly active in foreign intelligence and espionage. The agency operated a vast network of spies and informants in West Germany and other Western countries. The Stasi's foreign intelligence division, known as the Hauptverwaltung Aufklärung (HVA), was headed by Markus Wolf, one of the most effective spymasters of the Cold War. Under Wolf's leadership, the HVA successfully infiltrated numerous Western governments, military establishments, and intelligence agencies. One of the most famous cases involved Günter Guillaume, an East German spy who worked as a close aide to West German Chancellor Willy Brandt, leading to Brandt's resignation in 1974 when Guillaume's true identity was discovered.

The Stasi's influence extended into almost every sector of East German society. It had informants in factories, schools, hospitals, and universities, as well as in the arts and religious communities. The agency closely monitored intellectuals, artists, and activists, viewing any form of independent thought or expression as a potential threat to the state. The Stasi also infiltrated opposition groups and churches, often using informants to sow discord and prevent the formation of any organized resistance. The pervasive surveillance and control created an atmosphere of fear and mistrust, as people were constantly aware that they could be watched or reported at any time.

Despite its extensive surveillance capabilities, the Stasi faced significant challenges in controlling the population. The repressive nature of the regime led to widespread dissatisfaction and discontent among East Germans. Economic stagnation, lack of political freedoms, and the influence of Western media contributed to growing unrest. The construction of the Berlin Wall in 1961 was a stark symbol of the regime's efforts to prevent East Germans from fleeing to the West, but it also intensified the regime's control over its citizens.

The fall of the Berlin Wall in 1989 and the subsequent collapse of the GDR marked the end of the Stasi's reign. As protests grew and the regime's grip weakened, citizens stormed Stasi offices across East Germany, seizing files and demanding accountability. The extent of the Stasi's surveillance and repression was revealed as millions of files documenting the lives of ordinary East Germans came to light. These revelations shocked the public and led to a complex process of dealing with the Stasi's legacy, including the preservation and opening of the files for public access.

The aftermath of the Stasi's dissolution involved a complicated reckoning with the past. The German government established the Federal Commissioner for the Stasi Records, commonly known as the Stasi Records Agency, to manage and provide access to the extensive archives. Individuals could request to see their files, leading to personal reckonings with the betrayals and surveillance they had experienced. This process also had broader social implications, as it exposed the extent to which the Stasi had infiltrated society and the impact of its repressive tactics.

The legacy of the Stasi continues to be a topic of significant historical and cultural interest. The agency's methods and operations are studied as examples of extreme state surveillance and repression. The Stasi's tactics have been compared to those of other secret police organizations, such as the Soviet KGB, but its level of infiltration and the sophistication of its psychological operations are often seen as unparalleled. The Stasi's history serves as a cautionary tale about the dangers of unchecked state power and the ways in which surveillance can be used to control and manipulate populations.

In recent years, the legacy of the Stasi has also been explored through various cultural and artistic works. Films, books, and documentaries have depicted the experiences of those who lived under Stasi surveillance, providing personal insights into the psychological and emotional impact of the agency's operations. The 2006 film "The Lives of Others," which won the Academy Award for Best Foreign Language Film, is one of the most well-known portrayals of life under Stasi surveillance. The film's depiction of the invasive and oppressive nature of the Stasi's operations resonated with audiences and critics alike, contributing to a broader understanding of the agency's impact.

The history of the Stasi also has ongoing relevance in discussions about modern surveillance and privacy. The methods used by the Stasi to monitor and control the population have parallels in contemporary debates about government surveillance, data privacy, and the balance between security and civil liberties. The Stasi's extensive use of informants, psychological operations, and technological surveillance serves as a stark reminder of the potential for abuse when state power is unchecked and unaccountable.

Chapter 47: The Operation Fast and Furious

Operation Fast and Furious was a controversial and high-profile operation conducted by the Bureau of Alcohol, Tobacco, Firearms and Explosives (ATF), a federal law enforcement agency within the United States Department of Justice (DOJ). The operation, which began in 2006 and came to public attention in 2010, aimed to combat illegal gun trafficking across the U.S.-Mexico border. However, it quickly became notorious for its flawed execution and the subsequent scandal, commonly referred to as the "gunwalking" scandal, that erupted when it was revealed that the ATF had knowingly allowed thousands of firearms to fall into the hands of Mexican drug cartels.

The origins of Operation Fast and Furious can be traced back to a broader strategy aimed at addressing the flow of firearms from the United States into Mexico, where they were often used by violent drug cartels. The ATF, along with other federal agencies, was tasked with stemming this tide of illegal arms trafficking. The operation was part of Project Gunrunner, a larger initiative designed to disrupt the supply chains of firearms to criminal organizations. The specific goal of Fast and Furious was to identify and dismantle the networks responsible for purchasing and transporting guns to Mexico.

To achieve this, the ATF adopted a controversial tactic known as "gunwalking." This involved allowing known or suspected straw purchasers—individuals who buy firearms on behalf of others who are prohibited from doing so—to complete their purchases and then tracking the weapons to see where they would end up. The theory behind this strategy was that it would lead the ATF to the higher echelons of the trafficking networks, enabling them to gather evidence and make significant arrests. However, the reality of the operation diverged sharply from its intended objectives.

The implementation of Fast and Furious involved a network of gun shops in Arizona, where the ATF encouraged firearms dealers to sell weapons to individuals, they suspected of being straw purchasers. These dealers, who were often cooperating with the ATF, were assured that the agency was monitoring the situation and would intervene before the firearms crossed into Mexico. However, the ATF frequently failed to track the guns effectively, and many of them disappeared shortly after the initial sale. In total, approximately 2,000 firearms were allowed to "walk," including high-powered assault rifles and other deadly weapons.

As the operation progressed, it became increasingly clear that the ATF was losing control of the firearms. Agents expressed concerns internally about the potential consequences, but these warnings were largely ignored or dismissed by higher-ups who were determined to see the operation through. The fallout from this approach became tragically evident in December 2010, when Border Patrol agent Brian Terry was killed in a shootout in Arizona. Two of the weapons recovered at the scene were later traced back to Fast and Furious, bringing the operation under intense scrutiny and public outcry.

The death of Brian Terry was a turning point that led to a series of investigations and revelations about the true nature and extent of Operation Fast and Furious. The scandal garnered widespread media attention and prompted inquiries from both Congress and the DOJ. In February 2011, ATF whistleblowers testified before the House Committee on Oversight and Government Reform, revealing the details of the operation and its disastrous outcomes. These hearings exposed the deep flaws in the operation's design and execution, including the failure to adequately track the firearms and the lack of coordination with Mexican authorities.

The fallout from the scandal was severe and widespread. Several high-ranking officials within the ATF and the DOJ were implicated in the planning and oversight of the operation. Kenneth Melson, the acting director of the ATF, was reassigned, and other officials faced disciplinary actions or resigned. The controversy also reached the highest levels of the DOJ, with Attorney General Eric Holder coming under fire for his role in overseeing the department. Holder testified before Congress, denying prior knowledge of the specifics of Fast and Furious but acknowledging the need for better oversight and accountability.

In addition to the political and administrative consequences, the scandal had significant implications for U.S.-Mexico relations. The Mexican government, which had not been fully informed about the operation, expressed outrage over the influx of American firearms that had fueled cartel violence and contributed to the deaths of Mexican citizens and law enforcement officers. The lack of coordination and transparency between the two countries highlighted the complexities and challenges of addressing cross-border crime and gun trafficking.

Operation Fast and Furious also sparked a broader debate about gun control and firearms regulation in the United States. Critics of the operation pointed to it as evidence of the need for stricter laws and better enforcement mechanisms to prevent illegal gun sales and trafficking. Advocates for gun rights, on the other hand, argued that the operation was a case of government overreach and mismanagement, emphasizing the importance of protecting Second Amendment rights while ensuring responsible oversight.

The scandal had a lasting impact on the ATF and its operations. The agency faced significant reputational damage and underwent a period of introspection and reform. Changes were implemented to improve oversight and accountability, and new procedures were put in place to prevent similar operations from occurring in the future. The ATF also sought to rebuild trust with firearms dealers and the public, emphasizing the importance of collaboration and transparency in combating illegal gun trafficking.

In the years following the exposure of Operation Fast and Furious, numerous lawsuits and legal actions were filed by victims of the operation's failures, including the family of Brian Terry. These legal battles sought to hold the government accountable for the consequences of the flawed operation and to secure compensation for the harm caused. The ongoing litigation underscored the human cost of the scandal and the enduring need for justice and accountability.

Despite the extensive coverage and investigation, many questions about Operation Fast and Furious remain unanswered. The full extent of the operation's impact on gun trafficking and violence in Mexico is difficult to quantify, and the long-term effects on U.S.-Mexico relations continue to be felt. The scandal also serves as a stark reminder of the challenges and complexities involved in addressing transnational crime and the need for effective and ethical law enforcement strategies.

Chapter 48: The Arrest of Reality Winner

The arrest of Reality Winner in 2017 was a significant event in the annals of American intelligence and whistleblowing. Reality Leigh Winner, a former intelligence specialist and contractor for the National Security Agency (NSA), was arrested on June 3, 2017, and charged with leaking a classified document to The Intercept, an online news publication. This document, which detailed Russian interference in the 2016 U.S. presidential election, brought to light the intricate and often opaque workings of modern cyber-espionage and election meddling. Winner's arrest and subsequent legal battles underscore the ongoing tension between national security and freedom of information, as well as the personal cost borne by whistleblowers.

Reality Winner was born on December 4, 1991, in Kingsville, Texas. She enlisted in the United States Air Force in 2010 and served as a cryptologic linguist, a role that involved interpreting and translating foreign communications. During her time in the Air Force, Winner was stationed at Fort Meade, Maryland, where she gained experience in analyzing intelligence data. After her honorable discharge in 2016, she took a job as a contractor with Pluribus International Corporation, working at an NSA facility in Augusta, Georgia.

Winner's work at the NSA involved translating Farsi language material and providing analysis on intelligence related to Iran's aerospace program. However, her interest and involvement in issues of national security went beyond her official duties. She was reportedly disturbed by the political climate in the United States and the administration's handling of various issues. Her concerns came to a head in May 2017, when she accessed and subsequently leaked a classified NSA document that detailed Russian cyberattacks on U.S. voting software suppliers and local election officials.

The document, dated May 5, 2017, was an intelligence report that provided evidence of attempts by Russian military intelligence to compromise elements of the U.S. election infrastructure. Specifically, it described spear-phishing attacks targeting employees of a company that sells voter registration software and outlined efforts to infiltrate at least one American voting software supplier. This report added a significant piece to the puzzle of Russia's attempts to interfere in the 2016 election, confirming that the efforts were broader and more systematic than previously understood.

Winner printed the document and sent it anonymously to The Intercept. However, the process by which The Intercept handled the document led to Winner's exposure. The publication shared the document with government officials to verify its authenticity, inadvertently revealing tracking details that allowed the NSA to trace the leak back to Winner. On June 3, 2017, Winner was arrested at her home by FBI agents. She was charged under the Espionage Act, a World War I-era law that has been used increasingly in recent years to prosecute whistleblowers.

The Espionage Act does not distinguish between leaks to the press in the public interest and espionage for a foreign power. This legal framework meant that Winner faced severe penalties, including the possibility of a lengthy prison sentence. From the outset, her case was marked by controversy and debate over the treatment of whistleblowers in the United States, the transparency of government actions, and the balance between national security and the public's right to know.

Reality Winner's arrest and subsequent legal proceedings garnered widespread media attention and sparked a national debate about the role of whistleblowers. Supporters argued that Winner's actions, while illegal, were motivated by a genuine concern for the public good and the integrity of American democracy. They contended that the information she leaked was of critical importance to the public's understanding of Russian interference in the 2016 election. Critics, on the other hand, maintained that her actions had compromised national security and that she had violated her oath and the law.

Winner was denied bail on multiple occasions, with the judge citing her alleged flight risk and the seriousness of the charges. Her pre-trial detention was marked by significant stress and hardship, including solitary confinement and restricted communication with the outside world. Throughout this period, her legal team argued for her release and challenged the government's evidence, but to no avail.

In August 2018, Reality Winner pleaded guilty to one count of unauthorized transmission of national defense information. As part of a plea agreement, she was sentenced to five years and three months in prison, the longest sentence ever imposed in federal court for an unauthorized release of government information to the media. This sentence was seen by many as a harsh deterrent to potential whistleblowers and a statement on the government's stance on leaks.

During her incarceration, Winner was held at various federal facilities, including the Federal Medical Center, Carswell, in Fort Worth, Texas. Her time in prison was marked by continued advocacy from her family, legal team, and a growing number of supporters who viewed her as a political prisoner and a symbol of the struggles faced by whistleblowers in the United States. The hashtag #FreeRealityWinner became a rallying cry for those advocating for her release and greater transparency in government.

The broader implications of Reality Winner's case touch on several critical issues in contemporary American society. One of the most prominent is the tension between national security and freedom of the press. The document Winner leaked was undeniably of significant public interest, shedding light on a foreign power's attempt to undermine the democratic process. Yet, the severe consequences she faced for revealing this information highlight the risks and ethical dilemmas that whistleblowers encounter.

Winner's case also underscores the challenges of protecting classified information in the digital age. The ease with which sensitive information can be accessed and disseminated has increased the potential for leaks, but it has also raised questions about how best to safeguard national security without stifling transparency and accountability. The U.S. government's reliance on contractors, who may not have the same loyalty or oversight as permanent employees, further complicates this issue.

Another significant aspect of Winner's case is the legal framework used to prosecute her. The Espionage Act has been criticized for its broad application and the lack of distinction between different types of unauthorized disclosures. Critics argue that this law, originally designed to combat wartime espionage, is ill-suited to the modern context of whistleblowing and press freedom. The use of the Espionage Act in cases like Winner's has been seen as a tool to intimidate and punish those who expose government wrongdoing, rather than as a measure to protect genuine national security interests.

The personal toll on Reality Winner and her family is another important facet of this story. Her mother, Billie Winner-Davis, became a vocal advocate for her daughter, tirelessly campaigning for her release and raising awareness about her case. The human element of Winner's ordeal—the impact on her mental and physical health, the strain on her family, and the broader emotional consequences—adds a poignant dimension to the broader political and legal issues at play.

In the years since her arrest, Reality Winner's case has continued to resonate, particularly as debates about whistleblowing, press freedom, and government transparency have intensified. Other high-profile whistleblowers, such as Chelsea Manning and Edward Snowden, have similarly highlighted the complexities and consequences of exposing government secrets. Winner's case, however, remains unique in the severity of her sentence and the specific context of Russian interference in U.S. elections.

Chapter 49: The Assassination of Benazir Bhutto

The assassination of Benazir Bhutto, a prominent political figure and the first woman to head a democratic government in a majority Muslim nation, is one of the most controversial and complex events in recent Pakistani history. Benazir Bhutto was assassinated on December 27, 2007, during a political rally in Rawalpindi, Pakistan. This tragic event has been the subject of numerous investigations, speculations, and debates, particularly regarding the role of Pakistani intelligence agencies.

Benazir Bhutto's return to Pakistan in 2007, after years of self-imposed exile, was met with both enthusiasm and trepidation. She represented hope for many who desired a return to democratic governance and an end to the military-dominated political landscape. However, her return also threatened various vested interests, including those within the military and intelligence establishments, extremist groups, and political rivals.

The Pakistani intelligence community, primarily the Inter-Services Intelligence (ISI), has a long and intricate history. The ISI, established in 1948, has been deeply involved in domestic and international politics, often operating with a degree of autonomy and secrecy that has made it a powerful and sometimes controversial entity. Over the years, the ISI has been accused of meddling in political affairs, supporting militant groups, and maintaining an opaque relationship with various political leaders.

In the context of Benazir Bhutto's assassination, several theories and accusations have been levied against the ISI. One theory suggests that elements within the ISI viewed Bhutto as a threat to their influence and power. Bhutto had been vocal about her intentions to curb the influence of the military and intelligence agencies over the civilian government. Her close ties with Western nations, particularly the United States, and her stance against extremist groups operating within Pakistan were perceived as potential threats to the ISI's long-standing strategies and alliances.

On the day of her assassination, Bhutto was attending a rally in Rawalpindi, a city with a significant military presence. After addressing the crowd, she stood up through the sunroof of her vehicle to wave to her supporters. At that moment, a gunman fired shots at her, and shortly thereafter, a bomb exploded near her vehicle. Bhutto succumbed to her injuries and was pronounced dead shortly after.

The immediate aftermath of the assassination was chaotic and fraught with conflicting reports and theories. The Pakistani government, then under the leadership of President Pervez Musharraf, quickly pointed fingers at extremist groups such as al-Qaeda and the Pakistani Taliban. However, skepticism about the official narrative grew, especially given the contentious relationship between Bhutto and Musharraf's administration. Critics argued that the government was too quick to blame extremist groups and that the investigation lacked transparency and thoroughness.

Adding to the controversy, the crime scene was hosed down and cleared within hours of the assassination, a move widely criticized for destroying crucial evidence. This act fueled suspicions that there was a deliberate attempt to cover up the truth. Various independent investigations and reports have since suggested that the handling of the crime scene was either grossly incompetent or intentionally sabotaged.

In the years following the assassination, several reports and investigations have attempted to unravel the truth behind Bhutto's death. The United Nations conducted an inquiry into the assassination, releasing a report in 2010 that highlighted several critical issues. The UN report criticized the Pakistani authorities for failing to provide adequate security to Bhutto despite the clear threats against her. It also noted that the handling of the crime scene and the investigation was severely flawed.

The UN report did not conclusively determine who was behind the assassination but pointed to the likelihood of involvement by various actors, including elements within the Pakistani establishment. It highlighted that Bhutto faced threats from multiple quarters, including jihadist groups, political opponents, and elements within the security services who may have feared her return to power.

Adding another layer of complexity to the situation is the historical context of Pakistan's political and intelligence landscape. The ISI has often been seen as a state within a state, with its own agenda and operations that sometimes diverge from those of the civilian government. The agency's alleged involvement in political manipulations, coup plots, and support for certain militant groups has created an environment of mistrust and speculation. The ISI's opaque nature means that concrete evidence of its involvement in specific events, like Bhutto's assassination, is hard to come by, but the agency's history makes such suspicions plausible to many observers.

Moreover, Bhutto's assassination must be viewed in the broader context of Pakistan's turbulent political history. The country has seen numerous assassinations, coups, and political upheavals, often with alleged involvement or knowledge of its intelligence agencies. The political rivalries and shifting alliances within Pakistan make it a challenging environment to ascertain the full extent of any one entity's involvement in such events.

In the years following her death, Bhutto's assassination has remained a poignant symbol of the dangers faced by those who challenge entrenched powers in Pakistan. It underscores the volatile intersection of politics, extremism, and intelligence operations in the country. Despite numerous investigations and ongoing debates, the full truth behind Benazir Bhutto's assassination remains elusive. The legacy of her death continues to cast a long shadow over Pakistani politics, raising enduring questions about the role of the intelligence community in shaping the nation's political destiny.

Benazir Bhutto's assassination not only marked a tragic end to a significant political career but also highlighted the persistent challenges faced by Pakistan in establishing a stable and transparent democratic system. The incident remains a focal point for discussions about the power dynamics within Pakistan and the often murky operations of its intelligence agencies. It serves as a reminder of the complex and often dangerous interplay between politics and intelligence in a country striving to find its path amid numerous internal and external challenges.

Chapter 50: The Confession of Aldrich Ames

Aldrich Ames, a former CIA counterintelligence officer, orchestrated one of the most notorious and damaging betrayals in the history of American intelligence. His espionage activities against the United States on behalf of the Soviet Union and later Russia, resulted in the deaths of several CIA assets and caused significant damage to U.S. intelligence operations during the Cold War. Ames' confession and subsequent arrest in 1994 revealed a staggering level of treachery that exposed critical weaknesses within the CIA's counterintelligence and internal security measures, profoundly shaking the agency and leading to extensive reforms.

Aldrich Hazen Ames was born on May 26, 1941, in River Falls, Wisconsin. His father was a CIA analyst, which influenced Ames' decision to pursue a career in intelligence. He joined the CIA in 1962 and initially served as a records analyst. Despite a lackluster career marked by alcohol abuse and marital problems, Ames managed to secure important assignments, including a posting to Ankara, Turkey, in 1969. During his tenure in Turkey, Ames exhibited the first signs of susceptibility to compromise, struggling with financial difficulties that would later make him vulnerable to recruitment by foreign intelligence services.

Ames' downward spiral into espionage began in 1985, a critical year often referred to as the "Year of the Spy," due to the number of espionage cases uncovered. Desperate for money to support his extravagant lifestyle and his second wife, Rosario Ames, whom he met while stationed in Mexico City, Ames approached the Soviet Embassy in Washington, D.C., offering to sell classified information. The Soviets quickly recognized the value of Ames, who had access to highly sensitive information due to his position in counterintelligence, and they began to pay him handsomely for his betrayals.

Ames' espionage activities resulted in a catastrophic breach of U.S. intelligence. He provided the Soviets with the identities of virtually every CIA asset working in the Soviet Union, as well as numerous other top-secret operations. This led to the execution or imprisonment of at least ten CIA assets, including General Dmitri Polyakov, a highly valuable source who had provided critical intelligence to the United States for over two decades. The loss of these assets severely crippled the CIA's ability to operate within the Soviet Union and caused significant setbacks in American intelligence efforts during the latter years of the Cold War.

The initial signs of a mole within the CIA emerged as early as 1986, when the agency began noticing an alarming number of its assets being arrested or disappearing in the Soviet Union. The CIA launched an internal investigation but was unable to pinpoint the source of the leak. Despite the growing suspicion, Ames managed to evade detection for nearly a decade, partly due to the CIA's failure to thoroughly investigate its own employees and partly due to Ames' adeptness at covering his tracks.

Ames' lavish lifestyle eventually drew the attention of the FBI. Despite earning a modest government salary, Ames and his wife were living far beyond their means, purchasing a $540,000 house with cash, driving expensive cars, and wearing high-end clothing. In 1991, the CIA and FBI jointly reopened the investigation into the mole, focusing on Ames due to his conspicuous spending. By 1993, the FBI had amassed enough evidence to surveil Ames closely, including wiretapping his home and monitoring his financial transactions.

On February 21, 1994, Ames and his wife were arrested by the FBI. During the subsequent interrogation, Ames confessed to his espionage activities, providing a detailed account of his dealings with the Soviet and Russian intelligence services. His confession revealed the full extent of the damage he had inflicted on U.S. intelligence and the enormity of his betrayal. Ames was charged with espionage and sentenced to life in prison without the possibility of parole, while his wife received a five-year sentence for her role in his activities.

The Ames case had profound and far-reaching consequences for the CIA and U.S. intelligence as a whole. The breach exposed significant flaws in the agency's internal security measures and led to widespread criticism of the CIA's counterintelligence operations. In response, the CIA undertook extensive reforms to enhance its internal security, including more rigorous background checks, improved financial monitoring of its employees, and the establishment of a counterintelligence center designed to detect and prevent similar breaches in the future.

The damage caused by Ames' espionage extended beyond the immediate loss of human assets and operational capabilities. It also had a lasting impact on U.S.-Russia relations and contributed to a climate of distrust that persisted long after the end of the Cold War. The betrayal underscored the vulnerabilities inherent in human intelligence operations and highlighted the need for robust counterintelligence measures to protect sensitive information and personnel.

Ames' betrayal is often compared to other infamous espionage cases, such as that of Robert Hanssen, another FBI agent who spied for the Soviet Union and Russia. Both cases revealed significant lapses in internal security and underscored the ongoing challenge of detecting and preventing insider threats within intelligence agencies. However, the Ames case is particularly notable for the sheer scale of the betrayal and the devastating impact it had on U.S. intelligence operations.

In the broader context of espionage history, Ames' actions serve as a stark reminder of the complexities and dangers associated with intelligence work. The case illustrates how personal vulnerabilities, such as financial difficulties and marital problems, can create opportunities for foreign intelligence services to recruit insiders. It also highlights the importance of maintaining rigorous internal security measures and the need for continuous vigilance against potential threats from within.

The Ames case also had significant implications for the professional culture within the CIA. The agency was forced to confront its own shortcomings and take concrete steps to rebuild trust and integrity within its ranks. The reforms implemented in the wake of the Ames betrayal aimed to create a more secure and accountable environment, emphasizing the importance of ethical conduct and the severe consequences of treason.

Aldrich Ames' confession and the subsequent revelations about his espionage activities remain a seminal moment in the history of American intelligence. The case continues to be studied and analyzed for its lessons on counterintelligence, internal security, and the human factors that contribute to espionage. It serves as a cautionary tale for intelligence agencies worldwide, illustrating the devastating impact that a single individual's betrayal can have on national security and the critical importance of safeguarding against such threats.

Epilogue

As we conclude this journey through the hidden corridors of intelligence and espionage, we are left with a profound appreciation for the complexity and intrigue that define this shadowy world. The chapters in this book have unveiled stories of bravery, cunning, and sometimes moral ambiguity, revealing how clandestine operations have shaped the trajectory of history.

The world of intelligence is a dynamic and evolving landscape. Technological advancements, geopolitical shifts, and the ever-present human element continue to influence the strategies and outcomes of covert operations. The stories we have explored highlight not only the extraordinary feats of the past but also the ongoing challenges faced by intelligence agencies worldwide. The lessons learned from these historical cases remain relevant as new threats and opportunities emerge in our increasingly interconnected world.

Intelligence operations often operate in the gray areas of morality and ethics. The agents and operatives depicted in these stories navigated a delicate balance between duty and personal conviction, often operating under immense pressure and in extreme circumstances. Their actions, whether celebrated or condemned, were driven by a complex interplay of loyalty, fear, ambition, and necessity. These narratives compel us to consider the broader implications of intelligence work, reminding us that the pursuit of national security and strategic advantage frequently involves difficult choices and sacrifices.

As we move forward, it is crucial to recognize the importance of transparency, oversight, and accountability in intelligence operations. The covert nature of this work makes it susceptible to abuse and excess, as history has shown. Democratic societies must strive to balance the need for secrecy with the imperative of safeguarding civil liberties and ethical standards. The stories in this book serve as both cautionary tales and sources of inspiration, reminding us of the potential for both greatness and peril in the secretive world of espionage.

"The Secret History of Intelligence Operations" is a testament to the ingenuity, resilience, and complexity of those who operate in the shadows. Their contributions, often unsung and unseen, have played pivotal roles in shaping the world we live in today. As readers, we are invited to ponder the intricate dance between secrecy and truth, deception and revelation, that defines this clandestine realm.

In closing, let us carry forward the insights gained from these extraordinary stories. Let us honor the bravery and sacrifices of those who have walked the fine line between light and shadow. And let us remain vigilant, ever aware of the delicate balance that sustains our world, where intelligence and espionage continue to play a vital, if often invisible, role.

Thank you for joining us on this exploration of the secret history of intelligence operations. May these stories inspire curiosity, critical thinking, and a deeper understanding of the intricate forces that shape our world.

The End.